SOONER
THAN YOU
THINK

A PROPHETIC GUIDE TO THE
END TIMES

SID ROTH

DESTINY IMAGE® PUBLISHERS, INC.

P.O. Box 310, Shippensburg, PA 17257-0310

"Promoting Inspired Lives."

This book and all other Destiny Image and Destiny Image Fiction books are available at Christian bookstores and distributors worldwide.

Cover and interior design by Terry Clifton

For more information on foreign distributors, call 717-532-3040.

Reach us on the Internet: www.destinyimage.com.

ISBN 13 TP: 978-0-7684-0609-2
ISBN 13 eBook: 978-0-7684-0610-8

For Worldwide Distribution, Printed in the U.S.A.
5 6 7 8 / 19 18 17 16 15

SOONER THAN YOU THINK

DESTINY IMAGE BOOKS BY SID ROTH

Contents

Introduction

"I Am Coming Back Soon!"

Sid Roth

God says in the last days He will pour out His Spirit on all flesh and the old men will dream dreams (see Joel 2:28). That was talking about me. It seems like only yesterday I was a young Jewish man of thirty. I had just experienced the worst year of my life in which I had a horrifying encounter with Satan. Then I had a life-changing encounter with Jesus. I have never looked back, and now I burn with a passion and compassion for the lost.

I have had dreams from God that have made an impact on the world. In 1995 God instructed me in a dream to write a book of Jewish testimonies. He said more Jewish people would come to know Him through this book than anything I had ever done. He was right. We have distributed over 2.7 million of these books primarily to Jewish families in the United States, the former Soviet Union, and Israel. Only heaven knows the fruit of Jewish salvations from this God inspired book. To God be all the glory!

In 2013 I had another dream that rocked my world. Before the dream, if you had asked me if Jesus was coming in my lifetime I would have said yes, but deep in my heart I would not have been sure. Now all that has changed. I was not even thinking of the Lord's return when I had a vivid dream. God spoke to me three times and said, "I am coming back soon! I am coming back soon! I am coming back soon!"

Why would God tell me this? And, what does "soon" mean? In the *Merriam-Webster dictionary*, soon means: "in a short time after something happens." In this age of proliferation of nuclear arms, the world is on the verge of "something happening."

Jesus said about His return, *"But know this, that if the master of the house had known what hour the thief would come, he would have watched and not allowed his house to be broken into. Therefore you also be ready, for the Son of Man is coming at an hour you do not expect"* (Matthew 24:43-44).

How does Jesus warn us to be ready? He tells us to "watch." According to *Vine's Expository Dictionary*, the Greek word means to watch with vigilance and expectancy. I believe this prophetic guide will help you watch with vigilance and expectancy.

At the first coming of Jesus, my Jewish people studied the Scriptures in the original biblical language. And the amount of time the rabbis studied would put most Christians to shame in comparison. But still the majority missed the Messiah's first coming. What makes believers today so sure they will not miss the signs of His second coming? What if the end-time scenario we hold dear turns out to be wrong?

I do not want you to be caught by surprise. In Matthew 24:12 (NASB), Jesus says, *"Because lawlessness is increased,* **most** *people's love will grow cold."* Could it be that many of those who are so dogmatic about the order of end-time events have hardened their hearts to contradictory truth? Could most lose their faith if they go through tribulation or the rapture doesn't occur when they expect, or other end-time events unfold differently than what they have been taught?

In First Corinthians 13:9, Paul wrote, *"For we know in a partial, fragmentary, incomplete way, and we utter divine revelations in the same way."*[1] In other words we only see part of the picture through prophecy. Each one has part of the puzzle. But when we put the parts of the puzzle together, the picture comes into focus. Get ready to receive vital revelation for end times.

I have interviewed some of the best prophecy teachers and prophets over the years on television and radio. Now for the first time I am letting you see the whole picture by placing them in one book:

- Paul McGuire ("End-Times Previews") applies his journalistic expertise to some hard-to-understand aspects of end-times prophecy.

- Bill Salus ("Inevitable Conflicts") takes a look at the last wars before Jesus returns.

- L.A. Marzulli ("Great Deception") explains some of the basic issues that we encounter when we start to explore end-times prophecy.

- Perry Stone ("The Messiah Comes") explores the significance of the Jewish feasts in connection with the first and second comings of Messiah. Perry returns in another chapter ("Revelation about Revelation") that delves deeply into how we should look at Revelation, the premier book about the end times.

- Mark Biltz ("Divine Appointments") explains how biblical feasts are related to God's kingdom timetable, especially where the second coming is concerned.

- Tom Horn ("Prophetic Maze") connects biblical prophecy with current events to help Americans understand what is happening.

- Ann Rowan ("Pre-Tribulation Rapture") maintains that biblical prophecy points to a pre-Tribulation Rapture.

- John Shorey ("Mid-Tribulation Rapture? I Make My Case.") describes the seven events that must occur before the Rapture can take place.

- Ron Cantor ("Are You Ready for the Great Tribulation?") provides a clear exposition of the "post-Trib" view of the Rapture.

- David Brennan ("O, Jerusalem!") lays out vivid connections between events concerning Israel and end-times prophecies.

- Pat Schatzline ("The Remnant in the Last Days") affirms the importance of God's righteous remnant people in the end times.

- Dr. Jim Richards ("How to Prosper in the End Times") says God has a plan for you to prosper, even if there is a financial collapse.

- In the Conclusion, "Are You Ready for Your Final Day on Earth?" I explain how to make sure that you are ready for the end—regardless of how it happens.

Everything started in the tiny nation of Israel at the first coming of the Messiah. And everything will finish in Israel at His return. We know Jesus is coming back soon. This is the generation when the fig tree (which represents Israel) has blossomed (see Matt. 24:32). Israel has always been God's prophetic time clock!

Many have different views concerning when the return of Messiah will occur. In this book, you will read three different ways this could happen. Though they differ on *when* He will return, they all believe He is coming soon. The three most dominant views on the Rapture are the pre-Tribulation view, which teaches that the Rapture will occur *before* the Tribulation; the mid-Tribulation view, which claims the Rapture will take place in the *middle* of the Tribulation; and the post-Tribulation view, which says the Rapture will take place *after* the Tribulation. Since there is such division in the church on the timing of the Rapture, I have included the biblical case for all three views.

How could three people who love God and have studied the Bible on this subject come up with three different scenarios? Could it be that God has chosen not to fully reveal His end-times plan until the final generation? Could it be that we need all three end-times views to see the picture clearly? Daniel 12:4 (AMP) is about to come forth: *"...seal the Book until the time of the end. [Then] many shall...search anxiously [through the Book], and knowledge [of God's purposes as revealed by His prophets] shall be increased...."*

This is the Enoch generation! What were the two traits that Enoch demonstrated before he was raptured? He pleased God (obedience) and he walked in faith: *"It was by faith that Enoch was taken up to heaven without dying—'he disappeared, because God took him.' For before he was taken up, he was known as a person who pleased God. And it is impossible to please God without faith"* (Hebrews 11:5-6 NLT). My heart's desire for myself and for you is to so hunger for God that we become irresistible to Him.

In order for Jesus to say, "Well done" to us after we are caught up to be with Him forever, we must live a repentant life, love God and our neighbor, and walk by faith in His Word. I believe by understanding all three revelations of the Rapture taught in this book and walking a holy, biblically obedient life, we will be like *"...the sons of Issachar who had understanding of the times, to know what Israel ought to do"* (1 Chronicles 12:32).

My position has always been that I want to be raptured! Instead of being concerned with the timing of the Rapture, I concentrate on the parable of the ten virgins in Matthew 25. A virgin represents a believer. Five were wise and had enough oil to handle the darkness, and five were foolish and ran out of oil and missed the wedding.

Oil represents the Holy Spirit. I believe the only way we go up in the Rapture is to be filled with the Holy Spirit. This is achieved through intimacy with God. Jesus said it this way in John 17:3, *"And this is eternal life, that they may know You...."* The Greek word for "know" is a Jewish idiom for sexual intercourse between a man and woman. In other words, the purpose of eternal life is to have deep intimacy with God.

From within this intimacy, we can hear God and fulfill His purpose for our lives. The purpose of my life is to win souls. As the great German evangelist Reinhard Bonnke says, "I want to plunder hell to populate heaven." My issue has *never* been the timing of the Rapture or of the return of the Lord. I just want to be raptured, spend eternity with Him, and hear Him say, "Well done good and faithful servant." But my dream has given me insight into the timing of His return. He is coming back soon—sooner than you think!

In the meantime, until He returns, we are called to occupy. As things on earth appear to be getting darker and darker, God desires to flood you with His light. He wants you to be ready for the great end-times revival!

ENDNOTE

1.   Kenneth W. Wuest, *Wuest's Expanded Translation of the Greek New Testament* (Grand Rapids, MI: Eerdmans, 1958, 1994).

Chapter One

END-TIMES PREVIEWS

PAUL McGUIRE

I have studied many subjects, including history, and I do not think I have ever seen a time in history when so much biblical prophecy is happening under our very noses. (I don't want to say "before our eyes," because most people are missing it.) No matter where you go in the world, but especially in the First World nations, prophetic signs are appearing with increasing frequency. If you know what to look for, it can be both terrifying and exciting at the same time. More prophetic signs are coming true in our generation than ever before.

I'm not just talking about physical events such as storms and earthquakes, but also about economic and political developments, scientific advancements, and spiritual changes. The primary prophetic predictor has always been the nation of Israel, and, needless to say, that whole region remains particularly volatile.

WHAT DOES IT ALL MEAN?

One of those prophetic indicators is rapidly increasing knowledge, the overwhelming explosion of information across the developed world. The prophet Daniel spoke about this increase of knowledge in the last days:

> *But you, O Daniel, shut up the words and seal the Book until the time of the end. [Then] many shall run to and fro and search anxiously [through the Book], and knowledge [of God's purposes as revealed by His prophets] shall be increased and become great* (Daniel 12:4 AMP).

"Knowledge...shall be increased and become great." This implies an increase not only in the knowledge of God's Word and purposes and the created world in general, but also satanic knowledge—which works in both directions (the devil's knowledge about the children of God and our knowledge about his strategies). By implication, knowledge is *known*. It is not kept secret; just look at how knowledge is being disseminated much more widely than before.

Wireless and scaled-down communications devices used to be the stuff of science fiction. No one could have imagined how completely such communication (along with more fantastic-sounding means of transmitting information every year) could dominate modern culture.

As I study prophecy in the Bible, both the Old and New Testaments, I listen to the Holy Spirit. I want to investigate only what He directs me to investigate. I combine that spirit-to-Spirit attentiveness with a tremendous amount of research from mainstream sources. For me to be able to explain something to other people, it has to be thoroughly credible and documented. I end up gathering facts and figures about subject matter that I would normally never want to pursue, reading and studying extensively until I feel I have come up with something useful.

So, for example, as I explored the Scripture about the Tower of Babel (in Genesis 11) and Babylon in the Bible, I realized that this was the world's first one-world government, one-world religion, and one-world economic system. Then as I got into Revelation 13 and read about the one-world government, the one-world economic system, the one-world religion, a false prophet, and the Antichrist, I could see that both ends of the Bible covered the same idea—global government and global economy. In the system that Revelation describes, no one can buy or sell anything unless they have something called the "mark of the beast." And I began to put that together with actual developments in this world right now.

WHAT IS THE MARK OF THE BEAST?

Here's what John recorded in the book of Revelation:

> *He* [the beast] *required everyone—small and great, rich and poor, free and slave—to be given a mark on the right hand or on the forehead. And no one could buy or sell anything without that mark, which was either the name of the beast or the number representing his name* (Revelation 13:16-17 NLT).

> *Then a third angel followed them, shouting, "Anyone who worships the beast and his statue or who accepts his mark on the forehead or on the hand must drink the wine of God's anger. It has been poured full strength into God's cup of wrath. And they will be tormented*

with fire and burning sulfur in the presence of the holy angels and the Lamb" (Revelation 14:9-10 NLT).

So the first angel left the Temple and poured out his bowl on the earth, and horrible, malignant sores broke out on everyone who had the mark of the beast and who worshiped his statue (Revelation 16:2 NLT).

Then I saw thrones, and the people sitting on them had been given the authority to judge. And I saw the souls of those who had been beheaded for their testimony about Jesus and for proclaiming the word of God. They had not worshiped the beast or his statue, nor accepted his mark on their foreheads or their hands. They all came to life again, and they reigned with Christ for a thousand years (Revelation 20:4 NLT).

The Beast, of course, is the Antichrist, and the Antichrist is the great adversary of Jesus Christ who will arise in the last days. The Antichrist will embody satanic power to a degree never before seen in a ruler, and he will consolidate an unprecedented number of nations under him. Countless people will be deceived, thinking that this beguiling leader is not evil, but rather good-intentioned. "Peace" will be his byword. Somehow he will use a "mark" to identify the people held in his thrall.

> *The Beast is the Antichrist, and the Antichrist is the great adversary of Jesus Christ who will arise in the last days.*

I am convinced that we are coming into the time when we can anticipate what the mark of the beast will look like. Up until the second half of the twentieth century, people could only assume that the mark of the beast was some kind of indelible, visible, skin marking. Then burgeoning technological developments expanded the options, and improvements appear year after year.

The use of electrodes to measure bioelectrical signals goes back to the 1970s and earlier. After the terrorist attacks of September 11, 2001, the VeriChip Corporation, which for a time was combined with another company called Digital Angel, began to market tiny information microchips for people and animals. These radio frequency identification (RFID) chips are as small as a grain of rice, and they can be inserted under the skin and read with a scanning device. There microchips are considered a great idea for keeping track of elderly people with Alzheimer's disease, people with other health problems, children and celebrities who might be kidnapped, and animals that might be stolen or wander away. An ID number can be matched up with specific information that has been registered at a central location.

What part of the human anatomy is best for implanting these chips? Interestingly, they are imbedded most often either under the skin of the forehead or in the back of the right hand, which are the same two locations recorded in Revelation 13:16.

Similar to these imbedded ID microchips, some states now issue enhanced driver's licenses. These also carry an RFID chip, which transmits the license-holder's personal information up to a certain radius. A traffic officer or anyone who has the kind of monitor that can read the information can pick it up. You can see why people think this is a good idea, but it opens the way to the transmission of personal detail far beyond normal driver's license information. It would not be hard to have the transmitted information include your medical history, your religious and political affiliations, your arrest record, and more.

It's entirely conceivable that this information could be picked up and used against you. Let's say you are attending a pro-life rally or assembling for a cause such as traditional marriage. What's to prevent someone with a tracking device from sitting outside the meeting place in an inconspicuous vehicle, collecting information on every person who walks through the door: complete address and contact information, even a photo? By extension, IDs could be captured from Christians gathering to worship in a church or whatever. Phone taps and cell-phone data are nothing compared to what else is out there.

> *Your cell phone is essentially a tracking device.*

That being said, I hope you know that your cell phone is essentially a tracking device. Again, this seems like a good thing. If your phone has been stolen or you are lost in the wilderness, it's a great thing to be able to use it for tracking purposes. But even before cell phone technology became common knowledge, the Lord started talking to me about it. He told me that cell phones are for communication only secondarily, because their primary function would be as tracking devices. We forget how, in the early days of cheap cell phones, the screen would flash "GPS" (Global Positioning Satellite) when you would first turn it on. We hear about criminal cases in which evidence about location has been gathered from a cell phone, even when the power was turned off. It's only a step beyond that to access somebody's phone not only to establish its geographical location, but also to activate its camera and microphone functions to see and hear what's going on in the vicinity.

I realize that this sounds alarmist. I can hear the muttering among some readers, "Gee, this guy must belong to the tin-foil hat club." But all I'm saying is that this seems to parallel biblical prophecy about the end times, and that widespread, invasive surveillance is dangerously within the realm of possibility.

Under Surveillance Means Under Control

By reading basic technology manuals, you can find out how simple it would be to install a camera on the front of television screens as part of the manufacturing process; we already see webcams on our computer monitors. Conceivably, televisions or computers could then be commandeered for malicious information gathering, Internet broadcast, blackmail, harassment, or political control. All the time we are hearing about situations in which secret cameras and transmitting devices have been used to spy on people behind the scenes, including while they are within the privacy of their own bedrooms.

The average American does not realize that there is an actual science of mind control.

Even while most of us know that the capabilities of computer technology and biotechnology have gone through the roof, the average American does not realize that there is an actual science of mind control. Huge numbers of people, including political and cultural leaders, are at risk to be considered "Manchurian candidates" (a term taken from fiction about a brainwashed political candidate who is used by outside forces). This means that they have been programmed and they are not aware of it, and that devious forces will be able to make use of their influence. Eventually, unwelcome forces will gain control over the minds of an entire population.

If this sounds far out, just think of Adolf Hitler. I never wanted to read much about him until the Holy Spirit prodded me to do so. After many years of research, I began to realize that his ability to speak so powerfully and persuasively had a supernatural element. But it was more than that. It seemed to be advanced scientific mind control wedded to the supernatural power of occult. When Hitler spoke, people responded as if they had been mesmerized. They were willing to do things that otherwise would be repugnant to them. They believed what their leader told them and swallowed every falsification. Hitler learned how to use his vocabulary and body language to persuade the masses. His title, der Führer (the Leader) added to his ability to control the citizens of Germany and beyond. The symbols of the Third Reich are not accidental. They are occult symbols, and they incorporate mind control.

Your participation can be God-directed and God-protected if you pay more attention to His Word than the daily news reports.

As citizens and as Christians, we must guard our minds against unwanted influences, even when they come in handsome packages and win our trust with grandiose promises of prospective benefits.

URGENT—PREPARE WITH PEACE

You cannot prepare yourself if you do not know what is coming. The situation will only become more urgent, but your participation can be God-directed and God-protected if you pay more attention to His Word than you do to the daily news reports.

Those of us who have been equipped with a sort of prophetic radar need to keep warning those who do not have it. I know that after the 9/11 attacks, I was somehow able to sense the presence of terrorist cells in the continental United States. I couldn't tell specifically where they were located, but I could discern the general regions; I could feel their presence. And the Lord said, "Now you need to pray about it." The Lord has quickened me by the power of His Holy Spirit like a watchman, and when I see danger ahead, I sound a warning to the people of God.

I believe that a cataclysmic event is going to occur in the United States that will shake the nation to its very core.

In the near future, I believe that a cataclysmic event is going to occur in the United States of America that will shake the nation to its very core. People will be presented with a choice: they will have to choose either to follow God and His principles, looking to Him as their source of provision, protection, and deliverance, or they will have to choose to trust human government. As soon as anyone (including the Church) chooses to trust human government over God, they will be worshipping the spirit of Antichrist. By the time they find out that severe penalties will be incurred for their allegiance, it will be too late.

What will this cataclysmic event be? I don't claim to know. But it could be something such as multiple nuclear bombs being detonated in major U.S. cities simultaneously, or a major economic collapse. It could be an EMP (electromagnetic pulse) attack that knocks out the power grid and communications. Or it could be nuclear missiles fired from outside the country, perhaps even accidentally, that pierce the atmosphere in spite of the anti-missile system and wipe out a major U.S. city, mushroom cloud and all.

My goal is not to scare people, but to galvanize them to action. I want people to be prepared—and preparation starts in their hearts and minds. I want people to turn back to God and begin to pray as they have never prayed before.

The Bible says that judgment begins with the household of God (see 1 Peter 4:17). If you're looking for a way to forestall God's judgment, don't worry about the sins of non-believers. Instead look at the Church. If enough of us in the Church will repent, the Lord will drive back the powers of darkness and give us a temporary reprieve from the impending cataclysmic events. If we seek the face of God, He will pour out grace instead of judgment.

If enough in the Church repent, the Lord will drive back the darkness and grant a temporary reprieve from impending cataclysmic events.

We have not yet reached the point of no return, although we're dancing right on the edge of it. If we don't wake up and pay attention, we will blindly cross over that terrible line, and there will be no going back.

I'm not telling people to rush out and buy guns and stores of food and precious metals, but instead to store up the Word and the Holy Spirit. I believe that the Lord has given us one last, brief window of opportunity to seek His face and repent. If our repentance is genuine, and if we worship Him in spirit and in truth (see John 4:23), we will see the supernatural power of God released on America with such force that it will be like another Great Awakening. The fire of God will come.

I do not use those words lightly, because I have had personal experience with that fire. On a recent Fourth of July, my wife and I were reminiscing. About thirty-five years before, when we were dating, there was a great celebration for the Fourth in Manhattan during which time ships from around the world were gathered in the harbor. Suddenly I felt led to pray with her for America. So very calmly I began to intercede. I repented of my own sins and then I interceded and repented of the sins of the Church. Immediately and unexpectedly, I felt as though I had been set on fire by the power of God. I looked at the five fingers on each hand and they were burning hot, but I was not in pain. It was a supernatural burning. Then I could feel every cell in my body burning with fire. In the process, I was healed miraculously of a disease in my body. This was like a baptism of fire and it was a stronger experience than being baptized in the Holy Spirit.

It showed me once more that God is more powerful than any other force on the planet (or under the earth or above the earth). I want to be found on His side as the end times ramp up!

TOTALLY UNEXPECTED

I tell you, if God could get through to me, He can get through to anyone. I was not raised in a Christian home; I was taught that all answers to all questions can be found in science. I grew up in New York City, and I was not neutral about Christians—I hated them with such a passion that I would spit on the ground in front of churches on Sunday mornings. I called the people who worshipped there "idiots" and "hypocrites." Then in college at the University of Missouri, I remember arguing with two Christian girls in a debate class who were trying to convert me. I ripped their arguments to shreds and reduced them to tears. My college dual major was Film Making and—get this (realize that this was in the psychedelic 1970s)—Altered States of Consciousness. It was a brand-new field in the Department of Psychology.

So picture me as a kid with hair down to his belt buckle, cowboy boots, a two-pack-a-day cigarette habit, partying and dropping acid and rebelling in every way I could. But I was also an intellectual. I would read fifty books a week—philosophy and science and more.

I cannot emphasize strongly enough how much I hated Christians. To my mind, Christians were the worst of all religious people, lower than even the Hare Krishnas who used to dance in the airport. Yet I developed a strong attraction to the occult. I delved deeply into the New Age movement, communicating with spirit guides and all that.

Someone somewhere must have been praying for me.

But things began to fall together in a way that nobody could have predicted. Someone somewhere must have been praying for me. First, I kept running into Christians everywhere I went, although for the most part, my encounters just confirmed my negative impression of Christians. I even went to a Christian retreat with a geeky guy I ran into. I hated it so much, I hitchhiked back to campus. And what happened? Both of my rides were with Christians. The first car that stopped belonged to a Pentecostal preacher and his wife, and they began to witness to me.

My second ride was with a guy in a three-piece suit who was actually a Bible salesman; the back of his station wagon was packed with thick, black-leather-covered King James Bibles. Of course, he preached to me as he drove. No preliminaries, not even friendly. When he was done preaching, he looked at me and said, "You know, you are a sinner and unless you accept Jesus Christ as your Lord and Savior, you're going to spend eternity in hell." Now I didn't even believe in the word "sin." To me, sin was some kind of archaic concept. He invited me to pray the sinner's prayer, and he pulled off to the side of the road so I could repeat it after him.

Being from New York City, I fully expected to be the next victim of a traveling salesman ax-murderer, so I prayed the prayer. Of course I felt nothing different. But at least he didn't murder me. In fact, he drove me back to my campus, whereupon I went out and got drunk. But the next morning, bright and early, some Christian girls I knew rang the doorbell. I had always thought that one of the girls was especially cute, so I agreed to go out to the middle of campus with them, where I told them all about what had happened the day before. Then a girl I didn't know admitted that she wasn't sure if God was real, even though apparently she was a minister's daughter. And she looked me in the eyes and asked me, "Do you believe that Jesus Christ is the Son of God?"

> *For some strange reason, I blurted out words*
> *I had never said in my entire life, "I believe*
> *that Jesus Christ is the Son of God."*

For some strange reason, I blurted out words I had never said in my entire life, "I believe that Jesus Christ is the Son of God." The moment I said that, it was as if the sky literally cracked open and I could "see" God with my whole being. In that one moment, I knew that all the New Age stuff, altered states of consciousness, communicating with spirit guides, seeing the great white light, astral projection, all the gurus and their meditations—all of it was false. Only Christ was God.

And I have never changed my mind. That overwhelming experience set me on the journey I'm still on today. Not long after that, back in New York, I was baptized in the Holy Spirit in a way that was also overwhelming and humbling.

PROPHETIC RUMBLINGS

I went on to get married, have kids—and become a journalist. I poured my energy into researching, reporting, and writing; and for about a decade, I had my own syndicated, politically conservative radio talk show. All of that led into what I'm doing now.

In 1994, we were living in southern California when the devastating Northridge Earthquake hit. The earthquake measured almost 7.0 on the Richter scale and it injured and killed a lot of people. That was a key year for me, because I had written some books about Bible prophecy, although I must admit I had a cynical attitude toward that whole scene. Then when the earthquake hit in the wee hours of that January morning and it sounded like a locomotive smashing through our living room, my wife grabbed our three babies and we ran out into the street in the dark. All our neighbors had run outside too, and we congregated in our driveway, which was at the end of a cul-de-sac. Many of my neighbors were Jewish and many were non-believers. All they knew was that I was an author of books about biblical prophecy, so they kept asking me, "Are these signs of the times that Jesus talked about? Is this the end of the world?"

> *"Are these signs of the times that Jesus talked about? Is this the end of the world?"*

I think I was asked that same question a hundred or more times in the month that followed the earthquake. It was as if a veil was lifted from my eyes. Suddenly I realized that we really *are* living in the last days. I devoted the rest of my life to warning people and preparing them for what is happening and will be happening. I began to pay attention to prophetic stirrings myself so that I could be a better watchman. I also began to educate myself on topics that I never understood before, so I could teach people about what is going on.

I could fill up the rest of this book with facts and figures and informed opinions about the signs of the times and what we should be doing as we move forward. That's why I continue to write and speak. None of us should stop getting ready for the Lord's return, even if the whole idea disturbs us and we would like to get distracted from it.

I hope that it won't take another Northridge Earthquake, or something worse, to wake up the rest of the nation's Christians (and non-Christians, too). People are perishing for lack of knowledge. Nobody should be sitting on the fence about this. Fences are not safe anymore!

Take your Bible in one hand and the daily news in the other, and ask the Holy Spirit to show you what to do. In the name of Yeshua, the mighty Messiah, I pray that the power of God will descend on everyone who names His name. I pray that, infused with supernatural power from God, even the weakest person will become fearless like David when he faced Goliath, empowered by God's will and protected from any and all end-times calamities.

I pray that God, who is stronger than any scheme of the evil one, will give you peace in the midst of tumultuous times—and that you will be enabled to receive His peace and walk in it, straight to heaven's shores.

Chapter Two

Inevitable Conflicts

Bill Salus

The closer we get to the return of the Messiah, the more missing prophetic pieces come into play. A large number of those pieces have to do with conflicts in the Middle East, and God has focused my attention on that part of the world for more than a decade. The language of prophecy can be hard to interpret, but it can become a little easier if actual events begin to parallel what we read in the ancient words.

Often people wish that prophecies would read like news reports, but they don't. Instead of flowing logically and chronologically, and instead of naming things and places as we would name them today, prophecies follow rules of their own. Actually, they follow God's rules, and He is answerable to no one. He authenticates His sovereignty through the words that He speaks, and He speaks to inform us, not impress us. He wants us to seek His face when we hear or read His words. It's not that the Father has too much time on His hands, resulting in confusing and overabundant communications. Instead, He is the One who holds all time in His hands, and He wants us to participate in the unfolding of His eternal plan as we search out His intents and purposes.

God spoke about His prophetic word through Isaiah. He said:

> *Remember the former things of old, for I am God, and there is no other; I am God, and there is none like Me, declaring the end from the beginning, and from ancient times things that are not yet done, saying, "My counsel shall stand, and I will do all My pleasure"* (Isaiah 46:9-10).

Even though most prophetic words carry a sense of mystery and intrigue, and even though people tend to interpret them in many different ways, they are God's very Word. As Revelation 19:10 makes clear, they are the very testimony of the Word Himself, Jesus Christ. In the Revelation of John, the angel said, *"the testimony of Jesus is the spirit of prophecy"* (Revelation 19:10).

This fact makes prophetic words come alive, even when they concern people, places, and events that may be far away geographically or chronologically.

"IS THIS ARMAGEDDON?"

When the Twin Towers toppled on 9/11, God spoke clearly to me. It was a big wake-up call for a lot of people. I was asking Him, "What's going on? What is this awful thing? Is this Armageddon?" Many people were trying to answer that question. I remember hearing a well-known pastor say, "You need to focus on Ezekiel 38 and 39; that is what's going on." Those chapters are about Gog and Magog, and they portray a coalition of nine populations that many of us believe we can identify as Russian, Iranian, Turkish, Libyan, and more, that comes against Israel in the latter days.

But that's not what God said to me. He did not direct my attention to Revelation 16, either (about Armageddon). Many people were thinking that this was going to be the next war. Instead, God directed my attention to terrorism— what's feeding it and what will happen as a result.

The Bible has a lot to say about how terrorism came into being from the Arab-Israeli conflict, which is that unconventional method of warfare that the Arabs adopted after their conventional warfare failures of 1948, 1967, and 1973. What has become clear to me is that this conflict is going to come to a climax in the one that is described in Psalm 83. That major conflict is going to put everything else in place. Once that happens, the Israel that the Russian coalition is going to invade in the Ezekiel 38 picture, the nation that *"dwells securely in the last days,"* will have become a reality. Here is how the passage reads:

> *Thus says the Lord God: "On that day it shall come to pass that thoughts will arise in your mind, and you will make an evil plan: You will say, 'I will go up against a land of unwalled villages; I will go to a peaceful people, who dwell safely, all of them dwelling without walls, and having neither bars nor gates'— to take plunder and to take booty, to stretch out your hand against the waste places that are again inhabited, and against a people gathered from the nations, who have acquired livestock and goods, who dwell in the midst of the land"* (Ezekiel 38:10-12).

But Israel is not like that now. It is not dwelling securely without walls, bars, or gates, holding great wealth that Russia wants to plunder. This is not to say that Israel is not flourishing in many ways, because it is. Israel is blossoming in terms of things like the discovery of natural gas.

But the Israel that Ezekiel describes as dwelling securely—the little nation that is so prosperous that Russia forms a coalition to invade it for plunder—that kind of Israel does not exist right now. The reason is obvious: the very nations that surround Israel, which are listed in Psalm 83, want nothing more than to wipe Israel off the map. They fulfill the mandate of Psalm 83:4, which reads, *"They* [the enemies] *have said, 'Come, and let us cut them off from being a nation, that the name of Israel may be remembered no more.'"*

> *The very nations that surround Israel want nothing more than to wipe Israel off the map.*

I was so captivated with further revelation about how Psalm 83 fits into the context of current events that I wrote a whole book about it. Here is how the psalm reads:

> *Do not keep silent, O God! Do not hold Your peace, and do not be still, O God! For behold, Your enemies make a tumult; and those who hate You have lifted up their head. They have taken crafty counsel against Your people, and consulted together against Your sheltered ones. They have said, "Come, and let us cut them off from being a nation, that the name of Israel may be remembered no more."*

For they have consulted together with one consent; they form a confederacy against You: the tents of Edom and the Ishmaelites; Moab and the Hagrites; Gebal, Ammon, and Amalek; Philistia with the inhabitants of Tyre; Assyria also has joined with them; they have helped the children of Lot.

Deal with them as with Midian, as with Sisera, as with Jabin at the Brook Kishon, who perished at En Dor, who became as refuse on the earth. Make their nobles like Oreb and like Zeeb, Yes, all their princes like Zebah and Zalmunna, who said, "Let us take for ourselves the pastures of God for a possession."

O my God, make them like the whirling dust, like the chaff before the wind! As the fire burns the woods, and as the flame sets the mountains on fire, so pursue them with Your tempest, and frighten them with Your storm. Fill their faces with shame, that they may seek Your name, O Lord. Let them be confounded and dismayed forever; Yes, let them be put to shame and perish, that they may know that You, whose name alone is the Lord, are the Most High over all the earth (Psalm 83).

Those who have taken "crafty counsel" against Israel are terrorists. And terrorism is the ugly by-product of the Arab-Israeli conflict. The Bible speaks volumes about what follows.

It is an ancient hatred, and it has developed in a religious context. The Arab nations are largely Islamic, and this ancient hatred lies behind the policies of the nations of the Middle East. (The largest players are Iraq, Saudi Arabia, and Egypt, along with the Palestinians, Syrians, and others that share Israel's borders.) Many times over, skirmishes and clashes have erupted, sometimes escalating to the point of war. Peace talks always seem to fail. The bottom line is that the Arab-Israeli conflict can only get worse.

ROOTS OF THE CONFLICT

If you don't understand the roots of the conflict, you don't have a clue about what's going on, whether you are reading the news headlines or the Bible. It's like seeing the tip of an iceberg. If 90 percent of that iceberg is underwater and out of view, your decisions must be based on the scanty 10 percent that you can see with your naked eye, and inevitably those decisions will be faulty.

Six decades have passed since the reestablishment of the nation of Israel, and the conflict has become worse.

Six decades have passed since the reestablishment of the nation of Israel, and the conflict has become worse. Bible prophecy shows that it is not going to get any better. Now the enemies of Israel have more dangerous weapons than ever before, and they state outright that they want the Jewish state to be wiped out. This longstanding, ongoing conflict is going to play out in an Arab-Israeli war that was described about three thousand years ago by the psalmist named Asaph who was one of King David's worship leaders and who was also a prophet-seer.

This ancient hatred has been in existence from time immemorial, and it resurfaces perpetually. Hostilities erupt, with no apparent end in sight. It will not go away; it's cancerous; it needs surgical removal and unfortunately that means it must suffer the violence of war.

Why can people not orchestrate peace in order to avoid the horrible outcome? They have tried, but every attempt falls short. The only "peace plan" that could have worked has been breached, and that was God's peace plan. In Jeremiah 12, He put forth a plan for the peaceful return of the Jews to their land. But that would have required acquiescence from the Arab populations that were being displaced by the re-gathered nation of Israel, in other words a two-state solution, and they have not wanted it. Here is what God said through the prophet Jeremiah:

> *Thus says the Lord: "Against all My evil neighbors who touch the inheritance which I have caused My people Israel to inherit—behold, I will pluck them out of their land and pluck out the house of Judah from among them. Then it shall be, after I have plucked them out, that I will return and have compassion on them and bring them back, everyone to his heritage and everyone to his land. And it shall be, if they will learn carefully the ways of My people, to swear by My name, 'As the Lord lives,' as they taught My people to swear by Baal, then they shall be established in the midst of My people. But if they do not obey, I will utterly pluck up and destroy that nation," says the Lord* (Jeremiah 12:14-17).

HEZBOLLAH AND PSALM 83

Did you know that Hezbollah appears in Psalm 83? That terrorist organization is one of the players mentioned in verses 6 through 8, although not by its modern name. Those verses list the Arab populations that share a common border with Israel, and all you have to do is overlay the Old Testament maps with today's maps to figure out who the players are within their geographical regions.

> *The tents of Edom and the Ishmaelites; Moab and the Hagrites; Gebal, Ammon, and Amalek; Philistia with the inhabitants of Tyre; Assyria also has joined with them; they have helped the children of Lot* (Psalm 83:6-8).

The modern Saudi Arabians are here, and the Egyptians. Also the Jordanians—southern, central, and northern. Northern Iraq is represented. Last but not least, Lebanon and the Palestinian territories are covered in this list, which is where I see Hezbollah. Hezbollah is based in Lebanon, and has been heavily funded by Iran to resist Israeli occupation; it also receives significant political support from Syria. And presently the terrorist organization Hamas, an offshoot of the Egyptian Muslim Brotherhood, governs the Gaza Strip.

I do not think it was an accident when a thousand-year-old psalm book was discovered in 2006 in, of all places, an Irish peat bog. As it happened, this medieval psalter was unearthed by a bulldozer right in the middle of the 34-day conflict between Israel and Hezbollah that is now called the 2006 Israel-Hezbollah War. And the book was open to Psalm 83; it had been buried that way, which seemed portentous. That's why we saw headlines such as the one in the *Washington Post* that read, "Israel Mourns, Hezbollah Exalts." More headlines appeared in Israel. Psalm 83 is the only place in the psalms (not to mention the only place in the over 31,000 verses of the whole Bible) where you can find Hezbollah and Israel involved in a war.

Up until the time of that discovery, biblical commentaries had very little to say about the prophetic aspects of that particular psalm, which is now in the middle of finding fulfillment. Suddenly interest picked up.

UNITING ARAB STATES

A few years later, the "Arab Spring" rumbled to a start. This has created a very unstable situation in the Middle East with demonstrations and riots, governments being toppled, and radical elements seizing control. At first people thought it was nothing more than another social-media-driven youth uprising, and to Western eyes that seemed good because it sounded like "life, liberty, the pursuit of happiness." But the changes, which are still ongoing, have allowed militant forces to gain control in many places, and many of them are highly motivated to wipe out Israel.

The longstanding former leaders, regardless of their other faults, did not really represent an active threat to the state of Israel. Now the threats are real. New leaders who want to wipe Israel off the map have clout—and weaponry. The nation of Israel needs to be prepared for missile attacks, chemical weapons, and more.

Hezbollah launched thousands of rockets into Israel in the summer of 2006, and the civilians in northern Israel had to stay in their bomb shelters for more than a month. The United Nations issued a resolution that Hezbollah was supposed to dismantle the rest of the rockets, but now it seems that they have an arsenal of advanced Scud D missiles from Syria. This kind of missile can travel four hundred miles and hit within a twenty-yard target. This means that they could target anything from Israel's nuclear weapons power plant near Dimona to a crowded synagogue. During the summer of 2014, Hamas launched a multitude of rockets into civilian areas of Israel, including Tel Aviv. Thankfully, many were intercepted by the anti-missile "Iron Dome" defense system.

Psalm 83 shows united Arab forces coming against Israel—the ancient Arab hatred is still alive.

Although occasional conflicts break out between the Sunni and Shia Muslims, the Islamic states are generally more united than ever. Instead of fighting each other as much as they have done in the past, they are uniting around the common cause of promoting Islam. When Islam came along in the seventh century A.D., it started to unite them with common holy days and religious practices. Now part of the common cause is the destruction of Israel and its Western supporters. This implicates the United States, as we know from seeing our embassies attacked and threatened in country after country, including Libya, Egypt, Tunisia, and Yemen, along with watching an alarming rise in terrorist activity that has hit as close to home as 9/11.

Psalm 83 shows united Arab forces coming against Israel. The ancient Arab hatred is alive and they do not want Israel back on its land as it has been since 1948 when the modern nation of Israel was reborn.

I believe that Israel is on the brink of having to do something about Iran's nuclear program. Iran, as most people know, is the same as ancient Persia. And Persia shows up more than once in biblical prophecy. It's as though Iran has a dual role in the end-times scenarios. We see Persia involved in the Ezekiel 38-39 war with the Russian coalition of nations, and they also show up in Jeremiah 49:34-39 in a prophecy about Elam. Modern-day Iran is more than ancient Persia. Jeremiah identified them as Elam, which is western and southwestern Iran, along the Persian Gulf, where Iran's Bushehr nuclear plant is located today. Jeremiah warns that the Lord will strike them at the *"foremost of their might"* and *"break the bow"* of Elam (Jeremiah 49:35), scattering them so that there will be no nation where they don't go (see Jeremiah 49:36). The Elamites were expert archers. Could this mean that the nuclear plant will get attacked, and Iranians will be forced to flee in all directions because of nuclear fallout? I believe it could.

I do not know how imminent this event is, but I don't see anything standing in the way, especially in the light of Psalm 83, understanding what nations are involved. Peace talks have failed. Deals and sanctions have failed. Iran has nuclear power. Rockets have been stockpiled. The region is a tinderbox with an unprecedented potential for devastating upheaval.

DAMASCUS DESTINED TO DESTRUCTION—BY THE IDF?

Damascus claims to be the oldest continuously inhabited city in the world. It dates back to the time of Abraham, more than 4,000 years ago, and today it is home to more than one million Syrians. It also allows every known terrorist organization to set up shop inside its city limits. Someday, according to the prophet Isaiah, *"Damascus will cease from being a city, and it will be a ruinous heap"* (Isaiah 17:1). When you read the rest of the prophecy with current events in mind, you can see that it appears to be the Israel Defense Forces (IDF) that will have to destroy Damascus, in self-defense. It sounds cataclysmic: *"At eventide, trouble! And before the morning, he* [referring to Damascus by the personal pronoun] *is no more. This is the portion of those who plunder us, and the lot of those who rob us"* (Isaiah 17:14).

The Israel Defense Forces will play a key role in the fulfillment of prophecy.

The Israel Defense Forces will play a key role in the fulfillment of prophecy. In 1948, they were just a band of refugees. And yet when they came under attack, they won. In 1967, they won in six days. It happened again in 1973. Every time things flare up in a big way, they get stronger, and already some analysts rank their army as high as number ten in the world. Someday after they win what I call "the Psalm 83 war," I expect that they will be considered the *"exceedingly great army"* of Ezekiel 37:10.

It is interesting to note that Asaph wrote Psalm 83 long after the time of Gideon and also after the time of Barak and the prophetess Deborah. He included them in verses 9-12 as a warning and example of how God will deal with an Arab confederacy. Gideon's insignificant army of 300 men killed 120,000 Midianites after seven years of Midianite oppression (see Judges 7-8). The "Israel Defense Forces" of Barak and Deborah were empowered after twenty years of Canaanite oppression (see Judges 4). They won. And we never again find any such oppression over Israel in the Bible or historical record, not after those victories. They were decisive.

I believe that we are going to see that in this case. After the Psalm 83 war, those Arab countries will never again oppress the Jews in Israel. Then Israel will be able to dwell securely in the midst of the land, which will set the stage for the next big (Ezekiel 38) prophetic event. Naturally, even with the Psalm 83 devastation to the Arab world, the Arab populations will have a remnant, much like the Israelis have had and will have. I don't see any other way the prophecy about Damascus will be fulfilled than through a nuclear war. How else could Damascus cease to be a city overnight and become a ruinous heap?

This war may be soon, or it may not. Either way, it will not be a long war. Israel does not have the luxury of fighting a war of attrition, and they do not have a history of fighting protracted wars. The question is, will the next war be just another skirmish, or will it be a war of epic biblical proportions, the mother of all Middle Eastern wars?

WHAT ABOUT AMERICA?

How does all of this affect us in the United States? We have a large Jewish population, and the Arabs hate us as much as they hate Israel. Do we fit into the picture of the Psalm 83 war?

Needless to say, we cannot find our country mentioned by name in biblical prophecy. Gaza is in the Bible; Egypt is in the Bible; even Russia is in the Bible in our interpretation of the Gog and Magog scenarios. Some people argue that America could be something like the ten lost tribes or "Mystery Babylon" or the unnamed nation in Isaiah 18, but the real question is where we will be in the major war that is prophesied in Psalm 83, in view of the fact that America is Israel's best ally at this point in time. When we study Psalm 83, we don't see any involvement of foreign powers. Maybe we will have a supportive role.

> *God will bless those who bless the Jewish people, curse those who curse them.*

But I think that, considering biblical prophecy, we should be concerned about the future of America. We can no longer consider ourselves "America the Beautiful" and bountiful and blessed. We have forfeited our standing. The promise of Genesis 12:3 still stands: *"I will bless those who bless you, and I will curse him who curses you."* God will bless those who bless the Jewish people, curse those who curse them. While America has been the safest haven for Jewish people and a blessing to the formation of modern-day Israel, and while we can claim that God has showered His blessings on us because of this, God's hand of blessing seems to be pulling back. If our national stance is anti-Semitic, if we declare that the land of Israel should be divided and diminished as our president has said, what should we expect? Could this be why we are slipping away from being such a major world player economically in these last days?

The prophet Joel said that God judges nations for dividing up His land:

For behold, in those days and at that time, when I bring back the captives of Judah and Jerusalem, I will also gather all nations, and bring them down to the Valley of Jehoshaphat; and I will enter into judgment with them there on account of My people, My heritage Israel, whom they have scattered among the nations; they have also divided up My land (Joel 3:1-2).

America is playing with fire. We need to be on the right side of Israel in this upcoming war, or the curtain will fall on us at Armageddon.

Chapter Three

GREAT DECEPTION

L.A. MARZULLI

My interest in supernatural things started when I was a young man. I was raised Catholic, but I became disillusioned with Christianity as I knew it. So in the early 1970s, I became a devotee of Guru Maharaj Ji. As part of his orchestra, I went on a ten-city U.S. tour. Houston was one of the cities, and we were told that this was going to be a life-changing event. Well, it was, but not in the way I expected.

At the Houston Astrodome, a dais had been set up at the back of a big stage. On the dais sat the guru's "holy family," his three brothers and his mother. The guru (who was just a teenager) had a big crown thing on his head. The audience was applauding enthusiastically. I had to look behind me to see the family, because the orchestra was seated on the stage in front of them, and when I looked back, I was shocked to see that they no longer seemed quite human. I had no idea what I was looking at, but I figured, "Wow, this really is God! Look at this power!" I didn't have the discernment to tell whether the power was benevolent or malevolent, but I was overwhelmed. As a lot of people do when they see something supernatural, I had to assume that it was benevolent.

At the same time, it seemed kind of crazy, so not long afterward I left the organization and went into business. That didn't work out very well, either, and I kept checking out other gurus and things like Silva Mind Control and ESP. Then, when I was about thirty, I got hold of a book called *The Cult Explosion,* by a guy named David Hunt, and that turned out to be a game-changer. I found out a lot about the religious groups I had been involved with. And in the back of the book I found a little prayer, which I prayed out loud, adding: "Look, I don't know whether You're real or not, Jesus, but if You are, come into my life." I braced myself and kind of waited for something to happen, but it didn't.

The lack of evidence didn't mean that Jesus was not starting to do things in me. About a month later, I woke up in tears from a troubling dream, and at that point the Lord truly began to pull me out of the darkness of the evil one. It was a real battle, and it lasted a number of years. I began to be able to tell the difference between various kinds of spiritual manifestations, and this eventually led me into the full-time ministry I have today, in which I tell people how to spot deception and how to ascertain genuine signs of God's presence.

SIGNS OF THE TIMES

Most people recognize that supernatural activity is on the rise globally in unprecedented ways that are both encouraging and alarming. I try to investigate various supernatural manifestations, looking carefully at what is going on in various parts of the world in order to determine whether something comes from a good source or a bad one.

As a Christian, I always try to see how things line up with Scripture. Take Ezekiel 38, for example, which is a well-known prophecy about an end-times war. The prophet Ezekiel lived about 2,600 years ago, and yet he wrote prophecy that describes our world today with great specificity. For instance, he outlines a group of nations that will come in the latter days against Israel (which didn't end up being re-gathered from the four corners of the earth until 1948):

> ...Son of man, turn and face Gog of the land of Magog, the prince who rules over the nations of Meshech and Tubal, and prophesy against him. Give him this message from the Sovereign Lord: Gog, I am your enemy! I will turn you around and put hooks in your jaws to lead you out with your whole army—your horses and charioteers in full armor and a great horde armed with shields and swords. Persia, Ethiopia, and Libya will join you, too, with all their weapons. Gomer and all its armies will also join you, along with the armies of Beth-togarmah from the distant north, and many others.

> This is what the Sovereign Lord says: At that time evil thoughts will come to your mind, and you will devise a wicked scheme. You will say, "Israel is an unprotected land filled with unwalled villages! I will march against her and destroy these people who live in such confidence! I will go to those formerly desolate cities that are now filled with people who have returned from exile in many nations..." (Ezekiel 38:2-6, 10-12 NLT).

The leading nation is "Gog of the land of Magog." Many scholars of biblical prophecy identify Gog and Magog as Russia and/or Turkey. Now here we are at the beginning of the twenty-first century, and people are alarmed to see how Russia has its fingerprints all over the Middle East. (Just think about what has been happening in Syria and Iran.) This land in the "distant north" that Ezekiel writes about—could it be the same as the former Soviet Union that is supplying nuclear scientists for bomb-development in Iran and that always seems to appear in the midst of Arab uprisings? What we're beginning to see, in my opinion, is the formation of the Gog/Magog war that Ezekiel wrote about, because the nations he listed can be identified today. "Persia" was called that for thousands of years, although it is now called Iran. Ethiopia, Libya...we still see the same names.

These are strange bedfellows, but they will form a coalition and come against Israel, which Ezekiel calls *"an unprotected land filled with unwalled villages."* This is an unusual way to describe a nation, because unwalled villages would not have been common in the ancient world. In Ezekiel's time, even relatively small cities built the highest walls possible to keep out invaders. But with the advent of the airplane centuries after Ezekiel prophesied, as of the beginning of the twentieth century, that kind of protective defense became obsolete. Nobody could feel safe from attack anymore, even in a strong castle with walls and moats, because air raids can breach such simple defenses. It's just as if a land is filled with unwalled, undefended villages—just as Ezekiel put it. And over and over now, all eyes are on Israel as Iran and others threaten to wipe them out.

*Now, all eyes are on Israel as Iran and
others threaten to wipe them out.*

I am a watchman. I monitor all of this unrest, but I am not cemented in theological concrete. I know what the prophecies say and I keep a watchful eye on current events. We could be seeing a replay of the Six-Day War in 1967 in which Egypt and Jordan and Syria and all Arab countries came against Israel, and this may in fact lead to the Ezekiel 38 war. A watchman is supposed to wake people from their slumber or complacency and warn them of impending danger—and that is my role.

If you look at what is happening these days in Syria, it ties back to another prophecy, Isaiah 17:1, which predicts specifically that the city of Damascus will become a *"ruinous heap."* We didn't used to hear much about Damascus, but now the name of that city is in the news all the time because it is the capital of Syria. Nobody knows how it will be destroyed, but it does not stretch the imagination to think that it will be reduced to rubble at some point. Who knows? Perhaps the Syrian head of state will decide to destroy his own capital city.

The whole Middle East is volatile, and of course the news services could never cover all of it. I've never seen the region this unstable and pregnant with portent. Of course, unless you know the biblical prophecies about what will precede the Messiah's return, it will mean nothing to you. But when you begin to read these prophecies and then you see these nations begin to coalesce and form loose confederacies, you can only brace yourself for the inevitable war.

*When you read the prophecies and see these
nations coalesce and form loose confederacies,
brace yourself for the inevitable war.*

Of course for many Americans, this seems very far away.
For the most part we can't find ourselves in the Old Testament prophecies about the end times. But this does not mean
that the United States will be safe. I believe that the reason North America is not mentioned is simple—by the time
these wars begin in earnest, we will have been taken out of
circulation. It could follow any number of scenarios, such as
the detonation of an EMP (Electromagnetic pulse) weapon
a couple of hundred miles over the central part of the United
States. An EMP is basically a nuclear device, and it is common knowledge that Iran has been experimenting with this
idea. If they took one of their oil barges and retrofitted it
as a missile launcher, they could, from someplace like the
Gulf of Mexico, fire off a rocket that goes that high. They
could blast us back into pre-industrial times by disrupting
the entire electrical grid. Communications, transportation,
computers, refrigeration—all of it would be taken down.

Another way the U.S. could be taken out of the picture is
by seismic activity or volcanic activity. Already, we are seeing strong earthquakes happening around the planet every
ten or fifteen days. Is this business as usual, or is it something more? And volcanic activity—we have seen what
kinds of disruption an extra-big volcanic eruption can pro-
duce in terms of the viability of modern technology. Just
look what happened when the Eyjafjallajokull volcano in
Iceland erupted in 2010 and then again in 2011. It closed

the airspace over northern Europe for days. There is another volcano in Iceland called Grímsvötn that has a huge caldera. If that thing blows, or another supervolcano like the one under Yellowstone, it could put the entire planet into what is known as a nuclear winter. Crops wouldn't grow and a state of crisis would develop quickly.

Jesus Himself spoke about these times, saying, *"And you will hear of wars and rumors of wars. See that you are not troubled; for all these things must come to pass, but the end is not yet. For nation will rise against nation, and kingdom against kingdom. And there will be famines, pestilences, and earthquakes in various places"* (Matthew 24:6-7).

The predictions are subject to many interpretations, and none of us will understand their full implications until the events themselves unfold the rest of the way. I do believe that Christians will at some point be taken off the earth in what is known as the Rapture, but I don't know when that will be and I don't want to speculate on it. I also believe that there may well be "sanctuary cities" where Christians can gather together and somehow find divine protection, just as happened in biblical times. Even though my speculations get very specific at times, they remain just that—informed speculations. But I make every effort to speculate with a supernatural sensibility and, I believe, an amplified degree of discernment about good and evil compared to the average believer.

DEMONIC INCURSIONS

I feel that we have sort of dumbed-down supernatural experiences in American churches. We pride ourselves on being "with it," but we have established a fear of the supernatural because we don't want to look weird to out-siders—or to each other. But this fear-based ignorance could hurt us if something like the mark of the beast comes along. We could buy into it without feeling we were betray-ing Jesus.

What do I mean by the mark of the beast? This comes from the book of Revelation, which is the premier prophetic book of the Bible when it comes to the end times:

> *He* [the powerful and blasphemous "beast"] *required everyone—small and great, rich and poor, free and slave—to be given a mark on the right hand or on the forehead. And no one could buy or sell anything without that mark, which was either the name of the beast or the number representing his name* (Revela-tion 13:16-17 NLT).

In order to be allowed to buy, sell, or trade goods, people must receive the mark on their hand or forehead. At first, it will seem to be a good thing. But eventually, those who have taken the mark of the beast will long for death, but not be able to find it. They will end up with grievous sores on their bodies (see Revelation 16:2). And, without mercy, they will be punished by being thrown into the "lake of fire":

> *...Anyone who worships the beast and his statue or who accepts his mark on the forehead or on the hand must drink the wine of God's anger. It has been poured full strength into God's cup of wrath. And they will be tormented with fire and burning sulfur in the presence of the holy angels and the Lamb* (Revelation 14:9-10 NLT; see also Revelation 19:20; 20:10; 20:15).

There is a huge amount of speculation about what this mark of the beast could consist of. Is it a headband or wristband? A permanent mark on the skin such as a tattoo? Until we reached our current level of technological sophistication, we never could have imagined something like a computer chip being implanted just underneath a person's skin. But now, of course, medical people have the ability to do that, and such identification chips have become a viable option for people as well as animals.

> *There is a huge amount of speculation about what this mark of the beast could be.*

This touches on all sorts of things that relate to each other, and I don't have the space here to lay it all out completely. That's why I have written whole books about the Nephilim (the ancient race of giants in the Bible), and also about modern-day alien encounters. How does that relate to the mark of the beast?

The mark of the beast backstory involves what Jesus referred to as the "days of Noah" (see Matthew 24:37 and Luke 17:26). He said that His second coming would be like the days of Noah, but He didn't explain exactly what He meant by that. Still, if we look at the biblical account of the evil times leading up to Noah and the ark, when God destroyed all the evil living things on the face of the earth, we see that, interestingly, people had extended lifespans of hundreds of years. And we see this race of mighty giants that were purported to have come from the sexual liaison of fallen angels and human mothers (read Genesis 6).

In Genesis 6:4 (ESV), Moses writes that *"The Nephilim were on the earth in those days, and also afterward...."* We have always thought that the Flood put an end to them, but if Jesus says the days of His second coming will be like the days of Noah—and if we start looking at biblical history and prophecies about the conflicts leading up to His coming—we can see that there have been and will be further incursions of these strong human-seeming beings called the Nephilim.

Science fiction? I don't think so.

Basically, the Nephilim were demonic hybrids. We see more about them in the ancient book of Enoch, which is quoted seventy times in the Tanakh (the twenty-four books of the Hebrew Scriptures that form the bulk of our Old Testament) and the Nephilim are also alluded to in the books of Jude, Peter, First Corinthians, and in the Dead Sea Scrolls. These evil crossbreeds with extended lifespans were genetically manipulated from normal humans. I believe that the Fallen One (Satan) has been doing this over and over again throughout history. And any time the Nephilim are present, we see God's severe judgment. They get wiped out. This helps explain some of the most merciless judgments of God in the Bible, such as Sodom and Gomorrah.

Any time the Nephilim are present,
we see God's severe judgment.

Without having the Nephilim plugged into the narrative, the Sodom and Gomorrah story (complete with lake-of-fire brimstone) seems like genocidal overkill, especially coming from a loving, holy God. And later when Joshua and Caleb went in to conquer the Promised Land, this same loving, holy God told them to wipe out everything. It makes no sense—until you plug in the Nephilim. What a contrast to the way God treats, say, the city of Nineveh, whose inhabitants were notoriously depraved. To wicked Nineveh, God sent Jonah to extend grace and mercy. We just don't see that mercy being extended in cases where the Nephilim must have been present.

To my thinking, the connections are clear between the ancient Nephilim and the future divine judgment on those who have accepted the mark of the beast. The reason the recipients of this mark might long for death could be because the mark has altered them genetically, granting them overlong lives. Such longevity would be unwelcome in a time of upheaval and distress. This end-times war will be what some people call a "seed war"—a war between the seed of the Serpent/Beast and the seed of the Messiah. It's a gigantic cosmic chess match between the Most High God and the Fallen One, and the mark of the beast designates those who have sold out to the enemy.

> *Satan has been trying to foul up the image of God on earth since Genesis 6.*

The bottom line here is that Satan is always attempting to remake humankind in his own image. He is a counterfeiter. Humans have been created in the image and likeness of God. Satan's mission is to foul up the image of God on the earth, and that's what he's been trying to do since Genesis 6—with ever-increasing desperation.

THE GREAT DECEPTION

The final battle lines are being drawn up even now. What may be a key element in linking the ancient Nephilim to modern times has to do with credible (although often suppressed) reports of people who claim they have encountered aliens and UFOs, and that they ended up with some kind of miniaturized, computer-chip-type "thing" implanted in their bodies. This alien abduction phenomenon is not science fiction, either. I believe it is part of the Great Deception that the evil one is trying to pull off. For the most part, the people involved have been embarrassed to go public. Instead, they have sought out doctors who would agree to remove these devices surgically.

When the substance that one implant was made of was analyzed, it turned out to be closest to the meteorite metal found in places like that big crater in Arizona. The implant could not be pried open and was nearly impossible to cut open. A diamond blade saw in a machine shop couldn't crack it. Finally a laboratory cut it open with a laser beam. Viewing the inside through an electron microscope, analysts found nanotubes and double nanotubes, but they could not determine how they were supposed to function, nor how they got powered. Quite possibly, they are powered by the person's nervous and circulatory systems, and it seems likely they are capable of altering the host's DNA, which is startling, to say the least.

So, whether you want to call them demons or aliens, some kind of extraterrestrial beings seem to be showing up more often than they used to. I have interviewed many of the people who claim to have experienced encounters with UFOs—bizarre as it sounds, I know—and who have decided to talk about it. I have also interviewed one doctor who has removed these implants from people. This doctor did not know anything about eschatology, and he did not have an end-times "dog in the hunt" as Christians might. He said these implants are very complex, and they are giving off some sort of a frequency that seems to be one hundred times faster than our fastest computers. I asked him point-blank, "What do you think these things are doing?" and he answered me straight: "Well, they're changing the person's DNA." It sounds to me like the fallen angels mingling their DNA with the human genome. It's reminiscent of the days of Noah, which are differentiated from other times in history by the presence of the Nephilim. There could be a definite connection between the two.

> *Some kind of extraterrestrial beings seem to be showing up more often than they used to.*

When we read that Satan will be coming with deceptive signs and lying wonders (see 2 Thessalonians 2:8-10), why do we underestimate him? If we believe that supernatural phenomena come from somewhere and that they are real, whether benevolent or evil, why should it be so difficult to accept the outlandish idea that beings from "out there somewhere" have started to show up, along with the other earthly tumults that were foretold by the prophets of old?

Satan is the prince of the power of the air. Essentially, he has been sending aliens and UFOs to planet Earth since Genesis 6—and now he knows his time is short. We are building up to the consummation of this cosmic battle, and we should not be surprised that life is not business as usual. The enemy is ruthless and secretive. He wants to gather as many of the earth's people to himself as he possibly can, and in order to do it he will use lies and promises of world peace or whatever it takes. He will change human genetics to do it. He will disrupt communications and lay his own web across the face of the earth so effectively that by the time people wake up to what is happening, it will be too late to do anything about it. God is the only one who can bring Satan to his final end.

> *The enemy is ruthless and secretive. He wants to gather as many people to himself as possible and will use lies and promises of world peace or whatever it takes.*

Not many of these bizarre events make it into the news reports, but from time to time you hear of massive die-offs of birds or of cattle being mutilated without explanation. Of course you could say that some poison befouled the atmosphere or that some pranksters decided to slaughter farm animals in an abnormal way. Cattle mutilations have been going on for a long time, and yet law enforcement officials have not been able to bring anybody to trial. No footprints lead to the scene, even in fresh snow. A prize bull that was perfectly healthy the day before is found lying dead with his tongue and sex organ cored out with laser-like precision in a bloodless operation. It's as baffling as it is threatening. How could something do this? Did it just drop out of the sky into the middle of a farmer's field?

Sometimes people have reported seeing strange lights in the sky nearby. More than once, magnetic anomalies have been found around the dead animal, and even some kind of transmission chips have been found imbedded in the animal's flesh. What are we to make of this?

If we ever started hearing reports on the evening news of huge UFOs, don't you think people would get alarmed about it? Wouldn't they want to band together for safety, abandoning cultural and religious differences for the sake of self-preservation? Maybe reports are being suppressed and downplayed so that people *won't* do anything.

Actually NASA telescope photos have recorded changes in the sky—protrusions and strange movements around and within the moon and sun, although the offending images have often been redacted or erased from the final photos, probably because of policies based on avoiding an Orson-Wells-type induced panic in the general population. The Bible talks about changes in the sky as the time of the end approaches. Could this be what it means?

I can trace links between all of these things: aliens congregating and infiltrating humanity both in ancient times and now again in the present time, along with events that are too bizarre to be reported and threats that are too incredible for Western belief. Why have we not heard about most of this? I believe that because we're in the last days, things are coming to light for the discernment of those who are interested.

LIKE THE DAYS OF NOAH

Jesus was certainly not fearmongering when He said:

> *But of that day and hour no one knows, not even the angels of heaven, but My Father only. But as the days of Noah were, so also will the coming of the Son of Man*

be. For as in the days before the flood, they were eating and drinking, marrying and giving in marriage, until the day that Noah entered the ark, and did not know until the flood came and took them all away, so also will the coming of the Son of Man be. Then two men will be in the field: one will be taken and the other left. Two women will be grinding at the mill: one will be taken and the other left. Watch therefore, for you do not know what hour your Lord is coming. But know this, that if the master of the house had known what hour the thief would come, he would have watched and not allowed his house to be broken into. Therefore you also be ready, for the Son of Man is coming at an hour you do not expect (Matthew 24:36-44).

As you can see, Jesus was just trying to warn people to get ready. The most important issue is not whose interpretation of the signs is the most plausible. The issue is this—*"Are you ready?"* Jesus will be returning at an hour you do not expect. Will you be ready for Him? Have you been born again (in other words, has He made a supernatural change to *your* DNA)? Have you made Jesus your own Messiah and Lord? Have you asked Him to forgive your sins because He died for them, and to come live inside you?

> *The most important issue is not the interpretation of the signs. The issue is—"Are you ready?"*

It's not only plausible, it's feasible to be changed by means of a divine transaction. The only valid questions are: Who will be doing the changing? Who is your Lord?

Chapter Four

THE MESSIAH COMES

PERRY STONE

The Old Testament is filled to overflowing with buried treasures. In a multitude of ways, it reveals (although sometimes in a concealed way) both the first and second comings of the Messiah, Jesus Christ.

Primarily, of course, the Old Testament does it by means of a significant number of direct prophetic utterances recorded in the books of Isaiah, Jeremiah, Ezekiel, and other Old Testament prophets. Some have come true already—right down to the last detail—when Jesus came to Israel the first time. Others await their fulfillment. In addition, the Old Testament gives us foreshadowings and prophetic events. By reading the stories about what God has done in the past, we can discern how pivotal Old Testament events such as the Exodus from Egypt prefigure the coming of the Savior, the Lamb of God.

Yet another type of messianic foreshadowing comes through loud and clear—if you know what to look for. I'm talking about how the established feasts of Judaism, the annual round of ritual celebrations, tell about the Messiah, not only describing His first coming two thousand years ago, but also revealing His impending second coming. Jesus' first followers might not have entirely missed the significance of the Jewish feasts, because of course the majority of them were Jews. But as the Church abandoned Jewish traditions and developed new ones, we lost most of our awareness of the connections.

> *I want everyone to understand which*
> *of the feasts point to Jesus' first coming*
> *and which to His second coming.*

Our God is writing a seamless story. That's why we need to become familiar with the primary Jewish feasts in order to see the rich tapestry of meanings that they have for Christian believers today. I want everyone to understand which of the feasts point to Jesus' first coming and which to His second coming, so that we will not miss anything. Above, all, I don't want any of us to miss His return visit!

THE MOEDIM

The traditional feasts of Israel are known in Hebrew as the *moedim*. Corresponding to the seasons of the year, they are God's calendar for key events in the story of the Jews. There are seven primary ones, and a number of others. The seven are detailed in Leviticus 23 as "holy convocations," "appointed times" or "rehearsals" for the people of Israel, and they are to be celebrated in specified ways in order to provide both a history lesson and a picture of the days to come.

God doesn't say that these are feasts only for the Jews. In Leviticus 23, He calls them "My feasts." They reveal the truth of what will happen in the future, not only in the past. The springtime feasts reveal what would happen at Jesus' first coming, and the autumn feasts reveal what will happen at His second coming.

The springtime feasts include the Feast of Passover, the Feast of Unleavened Bread, and the Feast of Firstfruits, followed by the Feast of Weeks (Pentecost). Then there is a gap before the autumn feasts begin. They are the Feast of Trumpets, the Day of Atonement, and the Feast of Tabernacles. These seven feasts symbolize not only God's unfailing provision and protection from season to season, but also the complete redemptive story of Jesus Christ, starting with His death on the cross as the Passover Lamb and ending with His second coming, when He will come to dwell, or "tabernacle," with His redeemed people forever.

On the day of Pentecost, Peter spoke of a restoration of all things that have been spoken by the mouth of the holy prophets since before the world began, and it says this restoration will be a sign that Christ is about to be released from heaven to return to earth:

> But those things which God foretold by the mouth of all His prophets, that the Christ would suffer, He has thus fulfilled. Repent therefore and be converted, that your sins may be blotted out, so that times of refreshing may come from the presence of the Lord, and that He may send Jesus Christ, who was preached to you before, whom heaven must receive until the times of restoration of all things, which God has spoken by the mouth of all His holy prophets since the world began. For Moses truly said to the

fathers, "The Lord your God will raise up for you a Prophet like me from your brethren. Him you shall hear in all things, whatever He says to you" (Acts 3:18-22).

This restoration is always linked to Israel, to Jerusalem, and to the Jewish people because the Messiah is linked to them. The Gentile church has been grafted onto the Jewish root stock, and together we are spiritual heirs. The Jewish feasts have become ours.

SHADOW OF GOOD THINGS TO COME

For me, a revelation of the spiritual interconnectedness between the feasts and Jesus first occurred when I read about the "law" in Hebrews 10:1 with fresh eyes:

For the law having a shadow of good things to come, and not the very image of the things, can never with those sacrifices which they offered year by year continually make the comers thereunto perfect (KJV).

The Hebrew Torah, which we call the Pentateuch (the five books of Moses), lays out the law of God. I had always assumed that Jesus did away with the law. Of course He didn't; in fact, He proclaimed that He came to fulfill it: *"Do not think that I have come to abolish the Law or the Prophets; I have not come to abolish them but to fulfill them. For truly, I say to you, until heaven and earth pass away, not an iota, not a dot, will pass from the Law until all is accomplished"* (Matthew 5:17-18 ESV). If Jesus had done away with the law, He would have had to get rid of the Torah, which He did not do. If Jesus had gotten rid of the Torah, He would have eliminated all of its symbolism regarding His redemptive acts. He also would have abolished the entire ceremonial law of God, which includes not only the sacrificial law, but also God's moral law.

Jesus did fulfill the sacrificial part of the law; He accomplished it by His own self-sacrifice on the cross. However, the moral law (moral instructions and prohibitions) still applies to people today, as all disciples of Christ know. So when Paul says we're no longer under the law, he's talking only about the law of animal sacrifices for atonement for sin, not about the part of the law that says, "Do this" and "Don't do that." In fact, Jesus elaborated on the moral law, underlining its vital importance for receiving God's blessing. You can find the Law of Moses (the Ten Commandments) throughout the New Testament, because the law still applies for God's people.

We will never understand the return of Jesus if we don't understand the biblical feasts of Israel.

When Moses was on Mount Sinai (see Leviticus 7), God gave him the details of the entirety of the law and also the dates and the ritual observances entailed in the celebration of the seven primary *moedim*. Ever since then, in a seasonal cycle, the Jewish feasts have been highlighting and celebrating God's interactions with humankind and His intentions for the complete fulfillment of His law, which will not take place until Jesus comes again. This is why I saw that we will never understand the return of Jesus if we don't understand the biblical feasts of Israel.

SPRINGTIME FEASTS—
JESUS' FIRST COMING

The springtime feasts, four of them, walk us through the first part of the redemptive story. The first three feasts occur back to back.

The festival year begins with the Feast of Passover, which commemorates the Israelites' miraculous deliverance from death because of the lamb's blood on their doorposts (see Exodus 12). In the same way, believers in Jesus who are covered by the blood of the Lamb will be saved from spiritual death. The Last Supper was actually a Passover meal. In presenting the bread and the wine as His body and blood, Jesus identified Himself as the Redeemer, the ultimate Passover Lamb.

Immediately after the sun sets on Passover comes the Feast of Unleavened Bread, which recalls the hasty departure of the Israelites from Egypt, when they were in such a hurry that they could not wait for their bread to rise. Because the leaven represents sin, and also because Jesus is known as the Bread of Life (see John 6), the unleavened bread of the feast represents the Savior, who has no sin. He is unleavened bread for His followers.

Next comes the Feast of Firstfruits, which occurs at the beginning of the harvest time, a feast of gratitude for God's faithful provision. Ancient Israelites would bring a sheaf of grain or other firstfruits of their harvest, which would be waved before the Lord as an offering. Before the priest, they acknowledged that God had delivered them from Egypt, given them the Promised Land, and would continue to supply them and guide them. The Feast of Firstfruits reminds followers of the Messiah that just as He rose from the dead, becoming the *"firstfruits of those who have fallen asleep"* (1 Corinthians 15:20), so too shall every person who is born again in Him be resurrected in the last day.

After a gap of seven weeks (50 days) comes the Feast of Weeks, or Pentecost. (Pentecost means fiftieth day.) Celebrating the end of the grain harvest and also of the giving of the law to Moses on Mount Sinai seven weeks after the people of Israel left Egypt, the feast reminds Christians of the fulfillment of Jesus' promise to send *"another Helper"* (John 14:16, see also Acts 2:1-4), His Holy Spirit. The Spirit would be the guarantee of our salvation and future resurrection (see Ephesians 1:13-14). Fifty days after Jesus' resurrection, the Holy Spirit's coming on Pentecost confirmed the birth of the Church. So we can see how, to both Jews and Christians, Pentecost completes the redemption story that began on Passover.

Jesus was crucified on Passover, buried on the Feast of Unleavened Bread, rose from the dead on the Feast of Firstfruits, and sent the Holy Spirit on Pentecost.

The symbolism within these feasts is made even richer by the fact that Jesus accomplished vital steps of His plan on top of each of them. He was crucified on Passover. He was buried on the Feast of Unleavened Bread. He rose from the dead on the Feast of Firstfruits. And He sent the Spirit on Pentecost.

FALL FEASTS—JESUS' SECOND COMING

The feasts of autumn arrive after a four-month period in which there are no feasts. In the Middle East, these months, from early June until late September, are the driest ones, dividing the early rains from the latter ones. This jump in time between groups of feasts represents the church age, in which we find ourselves in the final stages today.

All three fall feasts come in the seventh month on the Jewish calendar. First comes the Feast of Trumpets, better known as Rosh Hashanah, which is the secular Jewish new year. Then after ten days comes the Day of Atonement, followed after only five days by the seven-day festival known as the Feast of Tabernacles.

These three fall feasts have not yet seen their prophetic fulfillment (except for the initial atonement of Christ through His death on the cross). They point to the future. Since the first four feasts have been fulfilled so magnificently through the events of Jesus' earthly life, we can look at the final three with absolute faith-filled hope and expectation.

Here is what the feasts encompass. The Feast of Trumpets designates the ending of the agricultural and the beginning of a sacred season in the festival year. Actual trumpets, ram's horns (shofars)—always a clear summons—ring out loud and clear at the outset of this feast, in effect summoning the workers from the harvest fields to the Temple for worship. The Feast of Trumpets is the rehearsal for that final trumpet blast, a picture of the great day of the return of the Lord, when the dead in Christ will be resurrected and the saints will be caught up and gathered together unto Him—the Rapture:

> For the Lord himself will come down from heaven with a commanding shout, with the voice of the archangel, and with the trumpet call of God. First, the

believers who have died will rise from their graves. Then, together with them, we who are still alive and remain on the earth will be caught up in the clouds to meet the Lord in the air. Then we will be with the Lord forever (1 Thessalonians 4:16-17 NLT).

Upon the return of the Lord, the spiritual harvest will be complete. The next feast is Atonement; the order of the feasts should help us anticipate the order of the unfolding developments after the Rapture. To the Jews, this is the time for God to judge Israel. Here are the Lord's words establishing the feast: *"Also the tenth day of this seventh month shall be the Day of Atonement. It shall be a holy convocation for you; you shall afflict your souls, and offer an offering made by fire to the Lord"* (Leviticus 23:27). For those who will have been caught up with the Messiah, it represents the period of time when they will be preserved from God's judgment of the world through the seven-year-long Tribulation.

The book of Revelation depicts three groups of people: those who are totally righteous, those who are totally unrighteous, and the in-between ones who will have to make an important decision. The totally righteous ones are represented by the 144,000 Jews who have been sealed by the angels of God (see Revelation 7:2-8). The totally unrighteous ones are those who do not repent of their evil deeds (see Revelation 14:9-11) and so they die lost. The in-between group are the ones who make their robes white in the blood of the Lamb (see Revelation 7:13-17). These are the ones who were not ready to be caught up at the return of the Lord, but they make a decision to serve the Lord and are willing to die as martyrs. (See Revelation 6:9-10 and 20:4.)

Five days after the Jewish Day of Atonement (prophetically, after the Tribulation), we come to the Feast of Tabernacles, which for those who have been saved means coming into the millennial kingdom of God. This is the season of our joy. In the traditional feast, Jews and Gentiles join together for a week of major celebrations, building booths to recall the temporary dwellings of the Israelites during their forty years in the wilderness. In the time to come, both the Jewish remnant and the faithful Gentiles will join together in the kingdom of God on earth. The King will rule from the city of Jerusalem; He will "tabernacle" with His people. The days of celebration are known as the Season of our Joy.

In the New Testament we read about how Jesus, on the eighth and final day of this feast, stood up and said, *"If any man thirst, let him come unto me, and drink. He that believeth on me, as the scripture hath said, out of his belly shall flow rivers of living water"* (John 7:37-38 KJV). His statement connected directly with something the priests would do during the Feast of Tabernacles. They would go down into a pool of "living water" (water flowing from a spring), wearing a golden vest, and they would scoop up some of the water. Then they would pour this water around the brass altar at the Temple, reciting from the Scriptures, *with joy we draw water from the wells of salvation* (see Isaiah 12:3). The rejoicing was intense on the last day of the Feast of Tabernacles, and so it will be in our eternal home with God.

The fall feasts are about rain and harvest. When Jesus comes back again, once and for all, He will send His angels with the sound of the trumpet to gather the saints who have survived the Tribulation from the four corners of the earth and bring them to the city of Jerusalem to worship Him.

THE MESSIAH REVEALED

The Jews' *moedim* include more than these seven primary feasts, and many of the traditions associated with the additional celebrations point clearly to the comings of the Messiah, Jesus.

Take Hanukkah, for instance. This eight-day festival that takes place in the middle of the winter is also called the Festival of Lights or the Festival of Dedication, and it memorializes the rededication of the Temple. You will be familiar with the nine-branched candlestick known as the *menorah*—a graphic representation of the lights. Part of the Hanukkah celebration includes a prayer. Interestingly, if you take the first letter of each of the first four words in Hebrew, they spell the Hebrew word for "Messiah."

Right at Hanukkah, Jesus proclaimed His standing as the Messiah, the Son of God, when He was within the actual Temple:

> It was now winter, and Jesus was in Jerusalem at the time of Hanukkah, the Festival of Dedication. He was in the Temple, walking through the section known as Solomon's Colonnade. The people surrounded him and asked, "How long are you going to keep us in suspense? If you are the Messiah, tell us plainly." Jesus replied, "I have already told you, and you don't believe me. The proof is the work I do in my Father's name. But you don't believe me because you are not my sheep. My sheep listen to my voice; I know them, and they follow me. I give them eternal life, and they will never perish. No one can snatch them away from me, for my Father has given them to me, and he is more

powerful than anyone else. No one can snatch them from the Father's hand. The Father and I are one" (John 10:22-30 NLT).

Another special holiday for Jews is Purim, which is based on the story of Queen Esther in the Old Testament. In the book of Esther, you can read the gripping account of how a young Israelite woman named Esther rose to the position of queen in Persia—just in time, as it turns out, to foil the plans of a wicked advisor named Haman who was trying to annihilate the Jews. As viewed through the lens of end-times revelation, Haman represents the Antichrist. The whole story is filled with symbolism about the Tribulation, redemption/salvation, and retribution against the enemies of God.

> *Every historical event in Israel's story, along with the commemorative holidays, is a portrayal of the grand finale of the world God created.*

In God's divine economy, every historical event in the story of Israel, along with its resulting commemorative holiday, becomes a portrayal of the grand finale of the world He created.

SEASONS AND CYCLES

In the Hebrew and also in the Greek view of the world, history was cyclical and therefore instructive for present and future reference. This way of interpreting historical events gives greater dimension to a study of the feasts and festivals of Judaism. As the preacher of antiquity put it:

The thing that hath been, it is that which shall be; and that which is done is that which shall be done: and there is no new thing under the sun. Is there any thing whereof it may be said, See, this is new? it hath been already of old time, which was before us (Ecclesiastes 1:9-10 KJV; see also Ecclesiastes 3:15).

In other words, in order to discover what's going to happen in the future, all you need to do is look at the past, because it will have occurred already at some point in time. History will repeat itself. Even in the life of Jesus, you can see repetitions and parallels. For example, the name of His earthly father, "Joseph," comes up again at the time of His crucifixion, when Joseph of Arimathea requests His body. When Jesus was born, a ruler named Herod was in power, and likewise at the end of His ministry. Jesus fasted for forty days at the start of His ministry, and He was seen alive for another forty-day period of time after He rose from the dead. Jesus ascended to heaven from the Mount of Olives, and He says that He will return to that same spot.

The past points to the future, and the future points back to the past. This way of looking at things helps as we sort out the significant symbolism within the divine-human drama.

> *The past points to the future, and the future points back to the past.*

When it comes to the feasts of Israel, centered as they are on seed planting, harvest, and rain cycles, the meaning is intensified. God has set these time frames out before humanity so we will pay attention to them. He wants us to know ahead of time how these facts point prophetically toward the future.

OUR ADVERSARY

Very few Christians understand the significance of the biblical feasts. Why is this? Quite simply, because we have an adversary—Satan. One of the historical details that amazes me is the number of times in the four Gospels that it was a feast day when Satan instigated his attacks on Jesus. He would either do it directly, or he would use people, especially the Pharisees. Skim through the Gospels and notice how many times attacks came against Jesus during Passover time, or around Pentecost, or at the time of the Feast of Tabernacles.

There must be something so supernatural about these feasts that Satan goes into overtime to hide their meaning from the Church.

WHERE ARE WE NOW?

We have seen how, from a prophetic prospective, the first four feasts, from Passover to Pentecost, found their fulfillment when Christ was here on earth. They bring us up to the birth of the Church in the second chapter of Acts, on the day of Pentecost.

We know we have not yet heard the trumpet call, so we have not arrived at the fulfillment of the fall feasts. But we know we're getting closer.

I would say that we're still living at Pentecost, because the outpoured Holy Spirit is still spreading throughout the world. As believers, we are still doing what Jesus told us to keep doing until He comes: we are preaching the gospel to the nations (see Matthew 24:14), participating in the work of the Spirit. Like Peter on the day of Pentecost, we are preaching Christ as our Passover Lamb, Christ resurrected from the dead, and Christ the Redeemer. We are preaching about how to be born again and enter into a redemptive covenant with Him.

In addition, we are looking into the future and preaching to people: "Christ is coming!" We can spy the Tribulation on the horizon. The kingdom of God is coming to the earth for good, and we must be ready.

We are still in what we call the church age. The Bible calls it the dispensation of the grace of God. The Greek word for "dispensation" is *oikonomia*, which is where the English word "economy" comes from. Scholars would explain it this way, that the Church has been assigned by the Lord to distribute and oversee the message of God's grace to the nations of the world. We are overseers or stewards of God's grace. We are the ones who show people the way. We show them how to be born again, and we explain what the covenant of God consists of. Then we say to them, "It's up to you. If you believe that this is true, you can be saved."

It feels as though the church age is a lot like the dry summer months in Israel. But as long as we are maintaining the outpoured grace of Pentecost, we're headed toward trumpets. There may not be a lot of rain right now, but as we get closer to the Feast of Trumpets, which is a picture of the Rapture, the atmosphere will begin to change. Just as it happens seasonally in the land of Israel, the clouds begin to form and the rain starts coming.

> *While our goal right now is to preach the*
> *gospel and experience the initial outpouring*
> *of the Spirit, there is more to come.*

This imagery helps the body of Christ understand that while our goal right now is to preach the Gospel and to experience the initial outpouring of the Spirit, there is more to come. Peter said (quoting from the second chapter of the prophet Joel), *"And it shall come to pass in the last days, saith God, I will pour out of my Spirit upon all flesh"* (Acts 2:17 KJV, see also Acts 2:16-21). As we get toward the last days, the days prior to Christ coming back to earth to catch up the saints, to what we call the Rapture, we can expect a magnificent final outpouring of the Spirit that will inundate the nations in what's called the latter rain. We're seeing the early stages of it all around the world now. It's clouding up and beginning to sprinkle.

Our task is to stay on track. We must stay focused on God's Word, obeying what He has told us to do. We must live for Him, and pray, and learn how to seek Him with all our hearts. Then (prior to the appearance of the "man of sin" that Paul describes in Second Thessalonians 2:3) we will be part of the greatest harvest of all time, which is the gathering into heaven of the saints of God.

Everybody who loves His coming—men, women, and children, Jew and Gentile—will go up to the heavenly Jerusalem to celebrate the fulfillment of the Feast of Tabernacles. Are you going to be one of them?

Chapter Five

DIVINE APPOINTMENTS

MARK BILTZ

If you have a keen interest in the prophetic timeline of the Bible and believe that God is the same yesterday, today, and forever, then you will discover within this chapter concepts that will revolutionize your walk as a believer in the God of Abraham, Isaac, and Jacob. What you are about to embark on will be one of the greatest revelations that have been revealed in these last days.

Fasten your seat belt as you go on the ride of your life. Many have found this information so eye-opening that common statements after understanding them include: "I've been robbed! Why has no one ever taught this? If only I would have heard this years ago!" Well, now is your time, let's get started!

The best place to start is always at the beginning. Especially since God declared the end from the beginning. Let's look at Genesis as to why God created the sun and the moon.

> *Then God said, "Let there be lights in the firmament of the heavens to divide the day from the night; and*

let them be for signs and for seasons, and for days and
years (Genesis 1:14).

A parallel verse we have to also begin with is from Leviticus:

Speak to the children of Israel, and say to them: "The
feasts of the Lord, which you shall proclaim to be holy
convocations, these are My feasts" (Leviticus 23:2).

I begin here because of the mistranslations in your Bible from Hebrew into English. When I read the word "seasons," I am thinking of winter, spring, summer, and fall. When I read the word "feasts," I'm thinking of food like a big thanksgiving dinner! But in Hebrew, seasons and feasts are the same word! They translated the same Hebrew word the first time as "seasons" and the next time as "feast." So what does the Hebrew word *moed* מועד actually mean, fall or food? Actually neither! More accurately translated this Hebrew word means "divine appointment," referring specifically to the important dates that God has put in His daytimer as to when He would intersect human history. God has a calendar that He uses and it isn't the one we use. Our pagan calendar is based totally on the sun. The Islamic calendar is based totally on the moon.

But God said, *"let them,"* so both the sun and the moon determine the seasons, days, and years. When the Bible mentions "seasons," it is referring to God's calendar as to when His divine appointments will be, such as Passover, the Feast of Trumpets, and the Feast of Tabernacles. When it says "days and years," it is referring to the biblical holy days, not our days of the week.

The term "years" refers to the Jubilee years occurring every 50 years and to the seventh year of the seven-year cycle known as the *shemittah* years when the land of Israel was to rest. It was also an economic reset year when debts were to be forgiven. The biblical calendar is the one that the Jews use as it is based on both the sun and the moon. The solar calendar is a great calendar as well as the Muslim lunar calendar, but they are not the ones that God uses on His prophetic calendar or for His prophetic time clock. When God sets His prophetic watch, it is according to His divine appointments or feast days that He predetermined as to when He will intersect with humankind. If you need to talk with someone in a different time zone, you have to agree on whose time zone you will use, or you will miss the call.

THE BIBLICAL CALENDAR

To demonstrate the importance for those involved with prophecy to be on the biblical calendar, let me give you a great example. In Zechariah it states:

> *Thus saith the Lord of hosts; The fast of the fourth month, and the fast of the fifth, and the fast of the seventh, and the fast of the tenth, shall be to the house of Judah joy and gladness, and cheerful feasts...* (Zechariah 8:19 KJV).

Here is a prophecy of four historic fast days that someday will be turned into feast days. If believers don't know when these occur on our regular calendar, we will never know when the prophecy is fulfilled. The fast of the fifth month is not in May! Most believers, due to the error of replacement theology and anti-Semitism within the church, have completely cut themselves off from the biblical calendar and completely severed themselves from anything to do with the Lord's own relatives, rejecting His own family. We have so distanced ourselves from His own culture that most have no clue of what month the fifth month is in His calendar or even the day the fast is and the entire meaning behind the circumstances of the fast.

> *Most believers have cut themselves off from the biblical calendar and severed themselves from anything to do with the Lord's own family.*

When we put these fast days on to our calendar, the historical perspective comes into view and we see how these are truly appointed times for God's people. The fast of the fifth month is on the ninth of Av, which falls around our August 9. This is the day Nebuchadnezzar burned the Temple to the ground. But it takes on greater significance when we see it is also the day the ten spies brought the bad report. It is also the very same day that Rome destroyed the Temple in A.D. 70. It is also the very day all the Jews were kicked out of England in 1290 and Spain in 1492. Not to mention that it is also the day World War I started and the very same day Hitler made his proclamation to kill the Jews. Are you beginning to get the picture as to why we need to put historical events from God's calendar onto our calendar?

So now let's go to God's appointed times during spring and fall, such as Passover, Rosh Hashanah and the Feast of Tabernacles and marvel at God's impeccable timing. Let's look at this next Scripture verse:

And all that dwell upon the earth shall worship him, whose names are not written in the book of life of the Lamb slain from the foundation of the world (Revelation 13:8 KJV).

This verse is telling us that Yeshua's (Jesus') death that would save humankind was planned from the very foundation of the world. It wasn't like the Father was taken by surprise when Yeshua died and quickly decided to go to plan B and resurrect Him.

PROPHETIC DRESS REHEARSALS

The Feasts of the Lord were also holy convocations. The Hebrew word translated into English as "convocation" implies more than just an assembly of people, it also is seen as a dress rehearsal. This is why the Passover lamb was slain every year on Passover. They did not kill it on some random day in August or December. These were not the feasts of the Jews but the Feasts of the Lord, and He determines when they are, not man. Not only did God preplan that the Passover Lamb (Jesus) was to be killed on Nisan 14, the day of Passover, but also that there was to be a daily morning and evening sacrifice that were to be performed at 9 a.m. and 3 p.m. So now the aspect of a dress rehearsal begins to come more into focus.

Every year on Nisan 14 at 9 a.m. the priest would bind the Passover lamb to the horns of the altar, and not only on the same day but at the very same time Yeshua was being bound to the cross. Did you know the Father even had King David—1,000 years before Messiah came—write what songs would be sung at His Son's funeral? Every year on Passover at 9 a.m. specific Psalms would be sung. The Psalms were the Israelites' hymnbook. They would sing Psalm 118. Josephus records there were two and a half million people in Jerusalem for the feasts. Can you imagine a choir of more than two million singing Psalm 118 that Passover morning at 9 a.m.? And what did Yeshua hear them singing?

> *God is the Lord and He has given us light; bind the sacrifice with cords to the horns of the altar* (Psalm 118:27).

By noon Yeshua had been lifted up from the earth and again they were singing Psalm 118. What were the words they were singing as day turns into night?

> *The right hand of the Lord is exalted; the right hand of the Lord does valiantly* (Psalm 118:16).

Amazingly, at 3 p.m. the time of the evening sacrifice, the Passover lamb would be slain—the moment Yeshua, our Passover Lamb, was slain! I pray you get hold of this truth. For 1,500 years Israel went through the dress rehearsal of killing the Passover Lamb on Passover! Messiah literally died on Passover, was buried on the Feast of Unleavened Bread, and He was unleavened or without sin. He rose on the Feast of Firstfruits becoming the firstfruits of the resurrection, literally on the Feast of Firstfruits!

The Holy Spirit was poured out on the Feast of Pentecost. Well guess what? Israel had been keeping the Feast of Pentecost every year for 1,500 years also! They were required to do so. That is why Jews from every nation were in Jerusalem at that time. Not only that, but in the book of Acts Peter said that the people were not drunk as it was only "the third hour of the day." That is 9 a.m., the time of the morning sacrifice! Another dress rehearsal! Did you know to this day many Jews still keep the Feast of Shavuot/Pentecost, staying up all night reading the Scriptures? I don't know any Pentecostals who keep the Feast of Pentecost.

Do you remember how the Lord told Moses to build the tabernacle based on the one God showed him from the heavenlies? Just as there is a Jerusalem on earth, there is a heavenly Jerusalem that God says will come down to earth (see Revelation 3:12; 21:2,10). I believe that what happens in the heavenlies results in an echo or a harmonic resonance happening on earth. What was happening on earth during the Old Testament was a shadow of the reality going on in heaven.

The Lord is the same yesterday, today, and forever!

So with this new understanding, do you realize the significance of the statement that the Lord is the same yesterday, today and forever? If this is true then if He fulfilled the spring feasts to the day of His first coming, He will fulfill the fall feasts to the day of His second coming! As it says in Ecclesiastes, there is a time and a season for everything; we need to know God's appointed times and seasons.

When the Bible talks about times and seasons, it is referring to the divinely appointed dress rehearsals. Yeshua rebuked the religious leaders of His day for not understanding this. All of creation obeys God and follows His instructions except humankind. The animals know when to migrate or to return home, but God's people lack understanding of when they are to return. Look at this verse:

> *Even the stork in the heavens knows her appointed
> times; and the turtledove, the swift, and the swallow
> observe the time of their coming. But My people do not
> know the judgment of the Lord* (Jeremiah 8:7 KJV).

God's people need to understand their appointed times if
they do not want to miss their divine appointment with destiny! Read this verse that explains it so well:

> *But of the times and the seasons, brethren, ye have
> no need that I write unto you. For yourselves know
> perfectly that the day of the Lord so cometh as a thief
> in the night. For when they shall say, Peace and safety;
> then sudden destruction cometh upon them, as travail
> upon a woman with child; and they shall not escape.
> But ye, brethren, are not in darkness, that that day
> should overtake you as a thief* (1 Thessalonians 5:1-4
> KJV).

God does not want us to be in darkness or for that day
to overtake us as a thief. So if the spring feasts speak of the
first coming of Messiah, what do the fall feasts speak of? If
the spring feasts were fulfilled to the day, what is supposed
to happen on the Feast of Trumpets, Yom Kippur, and the
Feast of Tabernacles?

Blessed are those who come in the name of the Lord.

Just as the spring feasts had to be fulfilled in order, it will
also be the same with the fall feasts. The Lord had to die
first on Passover before He could be buried on the Feast of
Unleavened Bread. He had to be buried before He could

rise on Firstfruits. He had to rise before the Spirit could be poured out in the Feast of Shavuot or Pentecost. Therefore the next feast to be fulfilled will be the Feast of Trumpets.

Is there anything written about trumpets in the book of Revelation? The Feast of Trumpets, also known as Rosh Hashanah, has many meanings and will have multiple fulfillments. I believe the Tribulation will begin some year on the Feast of Trumpets. This will be followed some year with the fulfillment of Yom Kippur, which is Israel's Day of Atonement. I believe some year on this day Israel will realize Yeshua is their Messiah. Then comes the fulfillment of the Feast of Tabernacles when Messiah will tabernacle on earth for a thousand-year reign of peace. Yeshua said to Israel, *"You will not see me again until you say, blessed is he who comes in the name of the Lord"* (see Matthew 23:39).

THE ULTIMATE WEDDING REHEARSAL

Are you excited about the coming of the Lord? Would you want to be at the wedding of the Messiah? Then why would you not want to attend the dress rehearsals? Follow along with me as we look at how the Scriptures relate the concept of a man and woman marrying to the Messiah marrying the Church:

> *For as a young man marrieth a virgin, so shall thy sons marry thee; and as the bridegroom rejoiceth over the bride, so shall thy God rejoice over thee* (Isaiah 62:5 KJV).

In other words, the wedding of the Messiah will follow the traditions of the Jewish wedding. So let's take a look!

> *Blow the trumpet in Zion, sanctify a fast, call a solemn assembly: Gather the people, sanctify the congregation, assemble the elders, gather the children, and those that suck the breasts: let the bridegroom go forth of his chamber, and the bride out of her closet* (Joel 2:15-16 KJV).

The Hebrew word for "closet" is better translated as *chuppah*. We see from the Strong's concordance: OT: 2646 closet /chuppah (khoop-paw'); from OT: 2645; a canopy.

A chuppah is what Jewish couples get married under. The parents often arranged marriages for their children like what Abraham did for Isaac.

Typically the young man would go to the house of the "bride-to-be" carrying three items: a large sum of money, betrothal contract, and a skin of wine. If the bridal price was approved, a glass of wine was poured. If she approved, the betrothal contract became a legal document between the two. Their status was betrothed rather than fully married even though they would be called husband and wife. We see this with Eleazer:

> *And the servant brought forth jewels of silver, and jewels of gold, and raiment, and gave them to Rebekah: he gave also to her brother and to her mother precious things* (Genesis 24:53 KJV).

The bride-to-be would be asked if she wanted to marry him, *"And they called Rebekah, and said unto her, Wilt thou go with this man? And she said, I will go"* (Genesis 24:58 KJV). The bride must give her "I do."

> *But what saith it? The word is nigh thee, even in thy*
> *mouth, and in thy heart: that is, the word of faith,*
> *which we preach; That if thou shalt confess with thy*
> *mouth the Lord Jesus, and shalt believe in thine heart*
> *that God hath raised him from the dead, thou shalt be*
> *saved. For with the heart man believeth unto righ-*
> *teousness; and with the mouth confession is made unto*
> *salvation* (Romans 10:8-10 KJV).

We see at Mount Sinai when God entered into the marriage covenant with Israel, they said their "I do."

> *And Moses came and told the people all the words of*
> *the Lord, and all the judgments: and all the people*
> *answered with one voice, and said, All the words*
> *which the Lord hath said will we do* (Exodus 24:3
> KJV).

At this time they would be engaged, in modern terminology, or as espoused.

> *Now the birth of Jesus Christ was on this wise: When*
> *as his mother Mary was espoused to Joseph, before they*
> *came together, she was found with child of the Holy*
> *Ghost. Then Joseph her husband, being a just man,*
> *and not willing to make her a public example, was*
> *minded to put her away privily* (Matthew 1:18-19
> KJV).

The bride and groom would be considered betrothed. This legally binds the two together, but they don't live together. A written document was drawn up called the *ketubah,* which states the bridal price, the promises of the groom, and the rights of the bride. The Bible is our *ketubah!* In it we find many promises, including:

> *For all the promises of God in him are yea, and in him Amen, unto the glory of God by us* (2 Corinthians 1:20 KJV).

> *And this is the confidence that we have in him, that, if we ask any thing according to his will, he heareth us: And if we know that he hear us, whatsoever we ask, we know that we have the petitions that we desired of him* (1 John 5:14-15 KJV).

Gifts were then given to the bride. And what do we find in the book of Ephesians?

> *But unto every one of us is given grace according to the measure of the gift of Christ. Wherefore he saith, When he ascended up on high, he led captivity captive, and gave gifts unto men* (Ephesians 4:7-8 KJV).

They would then share a cup of wine called "the cup of the covenant." Then the bridegroom would make the statement, "I will go to my father's house and prepare a place for her." This place was known as the chamber. This is what we find in the book of John that the Messiah said:

> *Let not your heart be troubled: ye believe in God, believe also in me. In my Father's house are many mansions: if it were not so, I would have told you. I go to prepare a place for you. And if I go and prepare a place for you, I will come again, and receive you unto myself; that where I am, there ye may be also. And*

whither I go ye know, and the way ye know (John
14:1-4 KJV).

If anyone would ask the bridegroom about the day of the
wedding, he would say, "Only my father knows"; for the
father had to be completely satisfied every preparation had
been made before the bridegroom could get his bride.

> *Messiah is preparing a place for you,*
> *that where He is, you may be also.*

A bridal price was also established for the bride. Accord-
ingly, we need to realize the great price that the Messiah
paid for His bride, the Church!

> *For ye are bought with a price: therefore glorify God*
> *in your body, and in your spirit, which are God's*
> (1 Corinthians 6:20 KJV).

> *Forasmuch as ye know that ye were not redeemed with*
> *corruptible things, as silver and gold, from your vain*
> *conversation received by tradition from your fathers;*
> *but with the precious blood of Christ, as of a lamb*
> *without blemish and without spot* (1 Peter 1:18-19
> KJV).

At this time the bride would have a *mikvah* or a water
immersion. It was a ceremonial act of separation showing
her going from a former way to a new way. We see this from
the book of Ezekiel:

> *"When I passed by you again and looked upon you,*
> *indeed your time was the time of love; so I spread*

> *My wing over you and covered your nakedness. Yes, I swore an oath to you and entered into a covenant with you, and you became Mine," says the Lord God. "Then I washed you in water; yes, I thoroughly washed off your blood, and I anointed you with oil"* (Ezekiel 16:8-9).

The bride now has been bought with a price and now she is to spend her time preparing to live as a wife and mother in Israel. She is to learn how to please her husband and wait for his return.

The bridegroom would return accompanied by a shout, "Behold the bridegroom cometh," and the Shofar was blown. This typically was done at night, which is why the lamps were always to be kept burning.

> *And at midnight there was a cry made, Behold, the bridegroom cometh; go ye out to meet him. Then all those virgins arose, and trimmed their lamps* (Matthew 25:6-7 KJV).

> *For the Lord Himself will descend from heaven with a shout, with the voice of an archangel, and with the trumpet of God"* (1 Thessalonians 4:16).

DRESSED FOR SUPPER

Finally there was the marriage supper for all invited. Can you imagine there are people who do not want to come to the supper?

> *Then said he unto him, A certain man made a great supper, and bade many: And sent his servant at supper time to say to them that were bidden, Come; for all*

things are now ready. And they all with one consent began to make excuse. The first said unto him, I have bought a piece of ground, and I must needs go and see it: I pray thee have me excused (Luke 14:16-18 KJV).

Let us be glad and rejoice and give Him glory, for the marriage of the Lamb has come, and His wife has made herself ready. And to her it was granted to be arrayed in fine linen, clean and bright, for the fine linen is the righteous acts of the saints. Then he said to me, "Write: 'Blessed are those who are called to the marriage supper of the Lamb!'" And he said to me, "These are the true sayings of God" (Revelation 19:7-9).

And Jesus answered and spake unto them again by parables, and said, The kingdom of heaven is like unto a certain king, which made a marriage for his son, And sent forth his servants to call them that were bidden to the wedding: and they would not come. Again, he sent forth other servants, saying, Tell them which are bidden, Behold, I have prepared my dinner: my oxen and my fatlings are killed, and all things are ready: come unto the marriage. But they made light of it, and went their ways, one to his farm, another to his merchandise: Then saith he to his servants, The wedding is ready, but they which were bidden were not worthy. Go ye therefore into the highways, and as many as ye shall find, bid to the marriage. So those servants went out into the highways, and gathered together all as many as they found, both bad and good: and the wedding was furnished with guests. And when the king came in to see the guests, he saw there a man which had not on a wedding garment (Matthew 22:1-5,8-11 KJV).

Amazingly, this story has connections with a prophecy in Zephaniah:

> *Hold thy peace at the presence of the Lord God: for the day of the Lord is at hand: for the Lord hath prepared a sacrifice, he hath bid his guests. And it shall come to pass in the day of the Lord's sacrifice, that I will punish the princes, and the king's children, and all such as are clothed with strange apparel* (Zephaniah 1:7-8 KJV).

Wow! God will punish His own children who do not come in a proper wedding garment. We need to understand these things if we want to be a bride without spot, wrinkle, or blemish.

AT THE VERY THRESHOLD

Now many are asking just how close are we to the coming of the Lord? What are the signs of His coming? I believe we are at the very threshold. This is based on the biblical fact of a day with the Lord being as one thousand years, and we are at the end of the sixth millennium since the creation of humankind. Another way of knowing is looking at Psalm 102.

> *You will arise and have mercy on Zion; for the time to favor her, yes, the set time, has come. For Your servants take pleasure in her stones, and show favor to her dust. So the nations shall fear the name of the Lord, and all the kings of the earth Your glory. For the*

Lord shall build up Zion; He shall appear in His glory
(Psalm 102:13-16).

The Hebrew word for "set time" is *moed*. On a feast day it will happen. The last statement says He will appear when Zion is being built up. Amazingly, in 1967 Zion was back in Jewish hands after 2,000 years! All of the bickering going on over Israel is because Jerusalem, or Zion, is being built up with all those settlements! Well look at the verse that follows:

This will be written for the generation to come...
(Psalm 102:18).

In Hebrew the word for "generation to come" is *acharone,* and means the terminal generation or the last generation. So the generation that sees Jerusalem being built is the generation that will see the Lord appear in His glory!

Yeshua rebuked the religious leaders of His day for not understanding the signs of their times and not realizing the day of their visitation. In Luke He told us in advance what the signs would be for His Second Coming:

Then He said to them, "Nation will rise against nation, and kingdom against kingdom. And there will be great earthquakes in various place, and famines and pestilences; and there will be fearful sights and great signs from heaven (Luke 21:10-11).

We have seen all of these in the past one hundred years. Look at what else He says:

And there will be signs in the sun, in the moon, and in the stars; and on the earth distress of nations, with perplexity, the sea and the waves roaring (Luke 21:25).

God specifically says there will be signs in the sun and the moon. I can't help but think of our original verse in Genesis and reread it with our new understanding. No wonder Yeshua said there will be signs in the sun and the moon when that is what they were created for! I will rephrase the verse with my own words for an even clearer meaning:

My paraphrase of Genesis 1:14: *And God said, Let there be lights in the firmament of the heaven and let them be for signs and signals when they occur on Passover, Rosh Hashanah, and Tabernacles!*

This is huge! The Creator of the universe wants to communicate with us, and the only way for us to realize the full ramifications is by knowing, following, and being on His calendar!

WHAT TO DO?

So what are we to do? I believe we are entering the "Super Bowl" of human history; and as Abraham, we need to be interceding for our nation. Do we want to be like Lot, totally intertwined with the society of our day that we are clueless to what God is saying? Or do we want to be like Abraham with whom God communicated to express His desire that a nation be spared?

In the Scriptures it declares God is looking for intercessors. But He is looking for intercessors who, like the children of Issachar, have an understanding of the times! In other words, those who are on His calendar!

*God is looking for intercessors who have
an understanding of the times!*

We live in such exciting times. We are the generation that may see the return of the Lord. Are we going to be like the dead church of Sardis where He will come as a thief in the night? Will we be like the sleeping church of Laodicea and not be watching eagerly for His expected return? Do we want to be like the foolish virgins or evil servants? Let's be like the wise virgins—alert and watching for the Lord's return and bringing as many as we can into His kingdom.

Chapter Six

REVELATION ABOUT REVELATION

PERRY STONE

The book of Revelation, which is the primary end-times book of the whole Bible, is hard to understand (to say the least). A blessing has been placed upon it for those who read and hear, but people have a lot of difficulty dealing with the large amount of symbolism. What are we supposed to do with a woman travailing in childbirth in heaven, who is clothed in the sun, has the moon under her feet, and has a crown of twelve stars on her head, and who eludes a great red dragon who wreaks violence? (See Revelation 12.) What do you think about a lamb who has seven eyes and seven horns? This is extreme, apocalyptic literature.

Of course, we can find plenty of symbolism throughout the Bible. Take Nebuchadnezzar's dream, for example, which we read about in the second chapter of Daniel. There we find an imposing statue composed of various metals, each representing a successive empire. These symbols are a kind of language, and in order to be understood, they need to be interpreted or translated.

One of the first things we learn about interpreting biblical imagery is that the Bible will always interpret itself. For example, because we see Satan in the form of a serpent in the Garden, we can expect that whenever a serpent appears elsewhere in the Bible, it represents Satan, sin, disobedience, or evil. And because the first mention of a lamb in an important role was the Passover lamb whose blood had significance, we can make the connection when John the Baptist introduces Jesus as the Lamb of God (and again in the book of Revelation where the word "lamb" is used twenty-seven times and all but one of them refers to Jesus Christ).

> *When interpreting biblical imagery, remember that the Bible will always interpret itself.*

The name of the book of Revelation in Greek is *apokalupsis,* which means an uncovering or unveiling or revealing—a revelation. It reveals things that have been concealed, but it does so with mysterious symbols.

MANY INTERPRETATIONS

The problem we encounter when we try to understand the book of Revelation is that people have come up with so many complex interpretations. Clearly, they can't all be right. And if all the experts can't agree, how can an ordinary Christian possibly know what to think?

As briefly as possible, let's just lay out the primary viewpoints about the Rapture, the second coming of Jesus, the Tribulation, and the millennial reign of Jesus. The viewpoints fall into two major categories: historical and future.

People who believe that the bulk of end-times prophecy has already been fulfilled by historical events are often called Preterists (from the Latin word *praeteritus,* which means "gone by"). Other people (like me) believe that biblical texts such as chapters 4 through 22 of the book of Revelation are yet to be fulfilled in the future. (A few people say that the Revelation is just an allegory about the heavenly Jerusalem, the earthly battle over the earthly Jerusalem, good versus evil, and God versus Satan.)

The specific details of these broad views are subject to endless speculation and theological interpretation. Although nobody can come up with an exact timetable for every event, I have studied the book of Revelation and other biblical prophecies my whole adult life, and have come to some firm conclusions about what we can expect—and what we should be doing about it.

Like many others, I cannot agree with the Preterist or historical points of view, which are held largely within the mainline denominations. I assure you that my reaction is not just a knee-jerk one, because I have delved so deeply into the subject matter. Noting the destruction of Jerusalem by the Romans in A.D. 70, Preterism says that all of the end-times prophecies were fulfilled in the first century. The historical interpretation holds that from the first century until the eventual return of the Christ, the words of the book of Revelation are gradually being fulfilled.

To my way of thinking, when an Old Testament prophet predicts that the sun will be darkened or the rivers will dry up, and I see a fulfillment of that word in the book of Revelation, it means that it has not happened yet. Historical fulfillment is not a possibility. The book of Revelation alludes so many times to the prophetic words of the Old Testament that it's difficult to count the references. Yes, of course some terrifying things transpired when the Romans destroyed Jerusalem and the Temple, but I believe that was only a major preparatory stage for the ultimate event.

> *The Preterists got the idea that all the signs of the Son of Man's appearing already happened from Jesus' own words.*

Where did the Preterists get the idea that all the signs of the Son of Man's appearing (wars, earthquakes, signs in the heavens, pestilence...see Matthew 24) already happened? They got the idea from Jesus' own words. Jesus had told His disciples, *"there are some of you standing here that shall not taste death till you see the Son of Man coming in His kingdom"* (see Matthew 16:28). Then once when they were gathered at the Sea of Galilee in Tiberius, Jesus predicted to Peter that he's going to live to be an old man (see John 21:18-19). Then Peter asked, "What about John?" (see John 21:21).

Jesus' reply is not definite. He says, *"What is it to you, Peter, if he is still alive when I come?"* (see John 21:22). Even the disciples misinterpreted what He meant, because the next verse reads, *"Then this saying went about among the disciples that that disciple should not die"* (see John 21:23). But Jesus never said John would not die, although we now know that he lived the longest of all of them. John ended up writing the book of Revelation when he was about ninety-five years of age and held in exile on the Isle of Patmos. He was the last of the original apostles; he out-lived all of them. In fact, all of them had been dispersed and most had died by the time Jerusalem was destroyed by the Romans.

And it's true that John did not die until he saw the coming of the kingdom of God—because of his kingdom revelation on Patmos. He saw the New Jerusalem that nobody else had seen. He saw the Lord coming back on a white horse as King of kings and Lord of lords. But that does not mean that all of the Old Testament prophecies were fulfilled within that short century. It most certainly does not mean that the church has replaced Israel in all of those prophecies, or that the Rapture is a fictitious notion.

People are just as mixed up as the Pharisees were in Jesus' time. The Pharisees were looking for a political leader with a religious slant who could overpower the Roman domination. Even the disciples were looking for this kind of an earthly kingdom. When Christ was going back to heaven, the last question they asked him was, *"Lord, will you at this time restore the kingdom to Israel?"* (Acts 1:6 ESV). Based on Old Testament prophecies, they knew that Israel was going to become a premier nation, that a king messiah was going to rule over Israel, and that Jerusalem would be the premier city among the nations' cities. They also knew that Jesus was the Messiah. So, basing their question on their assumptions, they expected Him to set up a political kingdom.

They missed the fact that the way the kingdom of God is now going to work is through the true church, the *ekklesia*, through believers, because it is not a political kingdom, but instead a spiritual one. Jesus came the first time as a lamb to suffer and to introduce His spiritual kingdom. But when he returns a second time, He will come as a lion—the lion of the tribe of Judah—to assume the political rulership of the planet.

> *The kingdom of God works through the true church—through believers.*

The kingdom that we are participating in is the spiritual one. That's why the Bible says, *"the kingdom of God is... righteousness, and peace, and joy in the Holy Ghost"* (Romans 14:17 KJV). God's Spirit dwells in individual believers and in the Church as a corporate body, and besides righteousness, peace, and joy, we see healing, deliverance from darkness, and salvation. Those who participate in this spiritual kingdom are bringing redemption to people. They are drawing them into a redemptive covenant with God so that they can become part of the kingdom of heaven. When the Messiah returns, they will become part of His kingdom on earth, which will persist for a thousand years (see Revelation 20).

People today have turned this around. They believe that the Church is going to grow to the point where it will take over the government, and that this is a progressive thing. Of course, any sensible person would like to see an army of righteous people take over the government, but I don't see it happening. If this were possible, I think that we would see more progress in that direction. Instead, in spite of having had three presidents who were in power for twenty-some years who believed that abortion was wrong, the law of the nation has not changed.

Yes, the kingdom is here now, in that believers pray and preach the kingdom message of the gospel of Christ to all the nations of the world, see people delivered from the hand of Satan and the power of death, hell, and the kingdom of darkness. But Revelation 19 has not happened yet, when the King himself will return at the end of a seven-year time of tribulation on the earth, arriving with the armies of heaven to set up an actual geopolitical kingdom on the planet.

RAPTURE: WHEN AND HOW?

The other thing that people are confused about is the what, when, and who of the Rapture. One of the complaints is, first of all, that the word "rapture" is nowhere to be found in the Bible. That's a fact. But it's also true that we use a lot of other words that are not in the Bible to describe spiritual realities. Take "Trinity," for example. You won't find it anywhere. Take "Millennial reign" or "Second Coming"; those terms are not there, although they come in handy for summarizing certain passages of Scripture.

"Rapture" comes from Saint Jerome's Latin translation of these verses:

> *For the Lord himself shall descend from heaven with a shout, with the voice of the archangel, and with the trump of God: and the dead in Christ shall rise first: Then we which are alive and remain shall be caught up together with them in the clouds, to meet the Lord in the air: and so shall we ever be with the Lord* (1 Thessalonians 4:16-17 KJV).

There's the phrase: "caught up." When the dead believers get raised up from mortal decay to immortality and assembled together with the firstborn in heaven, you could call that the "catching up" if you want to. But "rapture" conveys more accurately what it will be like when the saints are changed in the twinkling of an eye at the sound of the trump, meeting the Lord in the air and joining in joyful assembly in heaven.

Regardless of what you want to call it, the pattern of the Rapture can be found in Exodus 19, which tells about Moses climbing up Mount Sinai to a place where *"the Lord came down...and Moses went up"* (v. 20). He was surrounded by lightning, thunder, smoke, and a loud voice like a trumpet. Then He received God's revelation in the form of the Ten Commandments (see Exodus 20).

And then Paul himself, author of the letter to the Thessalonians, followed suit and went into Arabia (which is where Mount Sinai is) after his conversion (see chapters 1 and 4 of the book of Galatians). In Arabia, Paul received revelations much as Moses had; and when he returned, the first letter he wrote was First Thessalonians. In our Bibles, the letter is divided into five chapters. Paul mentions the return of the Lord in every chapter; but in chapter 4, he gives the church a new revelation about it—writing about the Lord descending from heaven and the saints being caught up to meet Him in the air. So this "catching away" teaching, or teaching about the Rapture, was the very first thing Paul explained to the church.

> *This teaching about the Rapture, was the very first thing Paul explained to the church.*

Israel knew that a messianic kingdom was coming. Zechariah had said that his feet would come to the Mount of Olives, that the mountain would split, and that the king would rule from Jerusalem. (See Zechariah 14:4-9.) But that's not what had happened when Jesus came the first time. Until Paul told them, nobody realized that there was going to be another return at which long-dead Christ-believers would be resurrected and the saints of God would be changed as they met the Lord in the air, that they would return with Him after the great judgment and after the marriage supper of the Lamb, in order to fulfill all of the Scriptures.

How will this fall out chronologically? If you put Daniel 9:27 together with Revelation 13:1, you can see that in the midst of a seven-year time of tribulation prior to the final return of the Lord, a treaty-breaker will arise. He is better known as the Antichrist. Where will the saints be when that happens? Will they have been caught up to heaven pre-Tribulation? Mid-Tribulation? Post-Tribulation?

PRE-TRIBULATION

I come down firmly in favor of a "pre-Trib" view. Based on intensive study of the Scriptures, I don't think we'll be here during the Tribulation. The early fathers of the Church seem to agree, because we do not see the Church anymore in the book of Revelation after the third chapter. We do see the "two witnesses" coming during the first forty-two months of the time of Tribulation, but we read in Revelation 11 through 13 (which portrays the middle of the tribulation period) that these two witnesses are killed. If the Church is on earth during those first forty-two months, why would we need the two witnesses at all? These two men (who may be Elijah and Moses) are the only ones declaring the gospel message during that time. If the Church were still present, we should see it preaching too, since we're supposed to preach the message of the kingdom until the end comes, according to Matthew 24:14. Then after the two witnesses are killed and raised back up to God in heaven, an angel comes down from heaven preaching the everlasting gospel and warning people not to take the mark of the beast. Not the Church—an angel.

> *Based on intensive study of the Scriptures, I don't think we'll be here during the Tribulation.*

Revelation 4 portrays a transition point. John heard a voice saying, "Come up hither," and he heard the voice of a trumpet. Immediately he was in the spirit in the heavenly throne room, where the elders and beasts were worshipping and a multitude is crying out, "You have redeemed us out of every nation!" Who else can that multitude be but the Church? Besides, when He came the first time, Christ told His listeners to pray that they would be counted worthy to escape all these things (trials and tribulations) and instead to be allowed to stand before the Son of Man. (See Luke 21:36.) The expectation seems to be that all believers will have been caught up (becoming part of that multitude in the throne room) by the time the Tribulation begins. Then, starting in the sixth chapter of the book of Revelation, we start to read about the Tribulation judgments being poured out.

CHRONOLOGICAL ORDER

We can figure out which theory is correct because the book of Revelation flows in chronological order. That's how I read it.

It remains chronological even as John jumps from heaven back to earth, under the earth, and then back to heaven again. He is seeing three worlds at one time. He has been told to show or write about the things that were, the things that are, and the things that shall be. The "things that were" can be found in chapter 1, where John saw Christ as the High Priest. The "things that are" would be the seven churches of Asia that were addressed in the individual messages. The "things that shall be" are still in the future tense. They are beyond the Church age. In the New Testament, the Church age is called *"the dispensation of the grace of God"* (see Ephesians 3:2), when the Church preaches the message of grace, mercy, forgiveness, and covenant for a long time. At the conclusion of that season, the overcoming Church will be "caught up." I use the word "overcoming" because John used the word so much. An overcomer is someone who follows the Lord, who has a covenant with Him, and who is looking for Him to return to the earth to accomplish His will.

Up to this point in John's Revelation, the Church is still on earth, still overcoming. But then comes the first verse of the fourth chapter: *"After these things I heard a voice like a trumpet saying, come up here."* That's all it takes. After the voice like a trumpet speaks, immediately we will be in heaven, just that quickly, just as it happened to John at that point. Then he began to describe what he saw, the Church's appearance before the heavenly throne.

What else can we see? Jumping ahead just a bit, we read, *"Now it's come time to judge the saints, the prophets, and those who fear his name"* (see Revelation 11:18). This is the fulfillment of what Paul spoke about in his letter to the Corinthians and also in his letter to the Romans. *"We must all appear before the judgment seat of Christ"* to receive rewards and crowns based on whether or not we did what God called us to do. This is in full operation in chapter 11—which happens to be in the middle of the Tribulation period. This means that the Church will be in heaven by that point. Chronologically, it's there, and a person who reads the book can't deny it.

Moving on, we come to the marriage supper of the Lamb (see Revelation 19). With a little background information about what the Torah says about newlyweds, and also about God's original pattern of taking a day of rest on the seventh day of creation, we can understand the marriage supper in a new way. In the book of Deuteronomy, a newly married couple was supposed to be given one year off to get to know each other. The man was not supposed to be sent to war within that full year. Now I believe that as the Tribulation is going on (see chapters 17 and 18), the marriage supper in heaven is also going on, and that it is one year long.

> *While the earth is gripped in the seventh year of Tribulation, the marriage supper of the Lamb is going to last the whole year.*

Considering that God worked six days when He created the earth, and then He rested on the seventh day, and considering that He established the jubilee law for the Israelites (six years of work earn a seventh year of rest), the principle holds for the work of tribulation as well. While the earth is gripped in the seventh year of Tribulation, the marriage supper of the Lamb is going to last the whole year.

Even Jewish weddings (think of Samson in the book of Judges or the wedding at Cana) lasted seven days straight.

In other words, the number seven is connected to the traditional Jewish wedding, and here the Church is the Bride of Christ. He is the Bridegroom. The seven days match up with the seven years that we will be in heaven with our bridegroom. Often there's a day for a year exchange in Scripture, so this is not a stretch to say.

For all these reasons, I believe that the Church will be caught up, or raptured, with Jesus before the seven-year Tribulation begins.

WHY BE CONCERNED ABOUT THIS?

With all of the end-times signs we can see—the restoration of Israel, the restoration of the city of Jerusalem, the nations aligning according to the words of the prophets—we need to be ready to be caught up and away. It's about to happen. How many of your friends and family members remain unsaved? How many have no interest in following Jesus?

John wanted the seven churches to understand how to live and how to overcome, and the messages he gave to those churches apply to us today. To this day, even people who seem to have no interest in the things of God start to get interested when they see how the prophetic words line up. The Holy Spirit opens up their understanding to believe.

I do not believe that there is very much holding back the Lord's imminent return.

I do not believe that there is very much holding back the Lord's imminent return. I see two major prophecies that must be fulfilled first. The first one is that the Church will have preached the gospel of the kingdom throughout the whole world. *"This gospel of the kingdom shall be preached in all the world for a witness unto all nations; and then shall the end come"* (Matthew 24:14 KJV). The message of the kingdom concerns both the first and second comings of the Messiah. Even as the message spreads and people receive it, the "fullness of time" is building. Only God knows when it will have fully come. Ephesians 1:9-10 describes how in the fullness of time, God will gather together His family in heaven and earth. Only God knows that time.

The second fulfillment to look for is the Holy Spirit being poured out on all flesh in the latter days, bringing people visions and dreams. (See Acts 2 and Joel 2.) This is happening to some extent already.

Despite the fact that some people believe the world is getting better and better and that we will be able to present it in a perfect condition to Jesus upon His return, what we see is a world that's getting worse and worse. Satan is still on the loose. We should not expect to see the fulfillment of Isaiah's visions (swords being beaten into plowshares, no more war, and the lion lying down with the fattened calf) until the thousand-year reign of Christ.

You cannot have a kingdom unless you have a king. There is only one King of kings and Lord of lords, and He is Jesus. He was called a great prophet when He was on earth. Presently, He is our High Priest in heaven. But the whole theme of the book of Revelation is the transference of Jesus from being High Priest to His full kingliness. Revelation 19 sees the coming of the kingdom rule of the Messiah. The timing for that transference depends on whenever the end of the seven-year Tribulation occurs. Then He will come back to earth with the armies of heaven (the saints who have been in heaven with him), and He will set up a visible, physical kingdom on earth. He will maintain the scars that resulted from His crucifixion just to prove that He is the suffering Messiah, worthy to become the King over the entire world.

Are you ready for this? With me, can you say, "May You come again, soon, Jesus! Catch us up with You and set about fulfilling every word You have ever spoken."

Chapter Seven

PROPHETIC MAZE

TOM HORN

End-times prophetic words include much more than the ones Christians typically cite from Old Testament prophets such as Isaiah, Ezekiel, Daniel, and Micah, or New Testament words spoken by Jesus or written by His disciples, including the book of Revelation.

In fact, alongside the earliest Jewish or Christian prophets, a complex web of predictions, divinations, and speculations has developed concerning the end of the world as we know it. Just because some of these come from ungodly sources does not invalidate them entirely. After all, just as Lucifer masquerades as an angel of light, so his demons can inspire prophetic statements that contain strong elements of truth, especially when they are viewed in conjunction with biblical prophecies.

When we observe clear connections between various prophetic sources, we should sit up and take notice. Who has influenced whom? What have been the results? How do symbols and symbolic language overlap? How often do Christians ignore the obvious (and alarming) network of links between prophecies, the facts of history, and current events?

What does it all mean, especially to American Christians in the tumultuous early decades of the twenty-first century?

PROTOTYPES AND PATTERNS

By definition, prophecies about the end times are about wars, dire judgments, disasters, cataclysmic events. They inspire fear. They make our heads spin. At the least, threatening revelations stretch our belief. Often we end up spending our energies contending with each other about whose interpretation is right, instead of looking for the kingdom of God in the signs of the times.

I prefer to spend my energies looking for evidence that matches reality. When I turn up new information about, say, the Mayan calendar (much in the news in 2012), I put it into the prophetic grid. When I see the connections between the predictions of the ancient Greek prophetess known as the Cumaean Sibyl and Freemasonry in Europe and America, I take notes. Having become familiar with the predictions attributed to the Irish saint named Malachy, news about the resignation of Pope Benedict XVI and his replacement, Pope Francis did not take me by surprise.

My radar keeps scanning for proof of what's out there. And it's been getting more interesting all the time.

NATIONAL AND SPIRITUAL INTERESTS

As an American, I am most interested in how developments within our influential nation will play out in end-times scenarios. Although Washington, DC, is probably not going to be a direct player at Armageddon, the connections are too numerous to ignore.

One of the clearest connections has to do with Freemasonry, which (interestingly, if you know what a "mason" does) has been built into the very foundations of our capitol.

As many as forty-four of the fifty-six signers of the Declaration of Independence were Freemasons. This doesn't mean that these founding fathers happened to be members of the same social club. They were members of a secret society which has, whether or not they realized it, evil origins and designs. By the vows they had taken, they were committed to building an occult form of democracy, one that would make itself large on the world stage.

By the time Freemasons have reached the highest ranking in the order, they have uttered many vows that bind them to demonic powers. Hidden under layers of symbolism and ritual is a very real supernatural authority that wants to infiltrate governmental seats of power so thoroughly that generations of citizens will simply consider its laws and values to be "normal."

We American Christians may talk about evil "powers and principalities" without realizing that we may be buying into some of their worldwide schemes. In fact, we may be "buying into" them every time we handle American currency, because of the symbolism that is inscribed on every dollar bill.

UNAVOIDABLE CONNECTIONS

Have you ever noticed the depiction of an Egyptian pyramid on the back of the dollar bill? It is part of the Great

Seal of the United States. The pyramid consists of thirteen steps, and its pointed capstone pictures the "all-seeing eye," which is supposed to indicate the favor of Providence on the nation. To the ancient Egyptians, the all-seeing eye was an emblem of Osiris, their omnipresent creator-deity, whom the Freemasons call the Great Architect of the Universe. The Egyptian god Osiris is the same as the Greek god Apollo.

And while the thirteen steps are meant to indicate the original thirteen colonies, they also carry other meanings. The number thirteen is significant in the 500-year-old Mayan prophecy that was talked about in the news in 2012, because that year was seen as the end of the prophecy's thirteen-step countdown that began in 1776. While the world did not end in 2012, that year could very well mark the end of an era before a new and final dispensation began.

The Latin words on the Great Seal include *Novus ordo seclorum*, a phrase taken from the *Aeneid*, the epic poem of the ancient poet Virgil and read by Christians since the Middle Ages as a prophecy (pagan but inspired) about the Second Coming of Christ. Virgil cites the "Sibyl," otherwise known as the Cumaean Sibyl, a priestess/prophetess of the Apollonian oracle, a major center of pagan prophecy at Cumae in ancient Greece.

Masonic symbols appear everywhere. You can go to the Library of Congress website and view an exhibit called "The Most Approved Plan: the Competition for the Capitol's Design" that goes back to how the plans for how the capital city would be built. After a variety of plans had been submitted, they were all rejected because Thomas Jefferson wanted a city-plan that would be based on the design in Rome. Specifically, he wanted to have a dome facing an obelisk—one that would be dedicated to all pagan gods. Here is a quote from the website: "The Roman Pantheon—the circular domed rotunda dedicated to all pagan gods—was suggested by Jefferson, who later shepherded it through several transformations."[1]

This domed rotunda symbolizes the ever-pregnant belly of Isis (Osiris' sister and consort) in Egyptian mythology, and an obelisk (which is what the Washington Monument is) represents Osiris' erect manhood, which the Egyptians designed to magically raise the spirit of Osiris from the underworld so that he could inhabit the Pharaoh and make him divine. The Romans adapted the stories to create their own mythology, and they used the imagery repeatedly in major cities of their empire. The obelisk you can see in all of the photographs of Saint Peter's Square in Vatican City is not a replica; it is a four thousand-year-old Egyptian obelisk, originally from Heliopolis, where it would have been dedicated to Osiris. So you see all kinds of unwelcome connections between ancient Egypt and Rome, the Vatican, Freemasons, and Washington, DC.

Even the Statue of Liberty is implicated. Gustave Eiffel (of Eiffel tower fame), who was a French Freemason, engineered its structural framework. According to the statue's background literature, "This colossal statuary follows designs going back to ancient Greek and Roman civilizations," and observers note the connections between the statue and classical gods.

We have been taught that the founding fathers were strong Christians, and that they founded the new country on Christian principles. But in fact most of them were Deists who had been influenced by the prevailing philosophies of the day. In brief, Deists believe that revelation and divine authority have been superseded by rational observation of the natural world, and that God is like a watchmaker who does not interfere in the day-to-day affairs of the world He created.

You can read about how George Washington's own pastor (although Washington rarely attended church) wrote in his memoir that as far as he knew, Washington was a really good man, but he was a Deist, not a Christian. We can look at Thomas Jefferson's personal Bible, from which he snipped out all of the accounts of Jesus' miracles and almost everything supernatural, including Jesus' resurrection. Ben Franklin belonged to secret societies on three continents, and he was a Grand Master of the Masonic Lodge of Philadelphia.

So you can see that occult elements have infused not only the seat and foundations of American government since 1776 (and I have only scratched the surface of the evidence), but also of all previous power structures of significance. As a nation, we have inherited and fostered a complex and diseased heritage.

> *In whatever guise, Osiris and Apollo are code names for the Antichrist of the New Covenant.*

Essentially, in whatever guise, Osiris and Apollo are code names for the Antichrist of the New Covenant. Apollo is named in the end-times visions of the book of Revelation. ("Apollyon" is a transliteration of the Greek):

> *And the fifth angel sounded, and I saw a star fall from heaven unto the earth: and to him was given the key*

of the bottomless pit. And there came out of the smoke locusts upon the earth: and unto them was given power, as the scorpions of the earth have power. And they had tails like unto scorpions, and there were stings in their tails: and their power was to hurt men five months. And they had a king over them, which is the angel of the bottomless pit, whose name in the Hebrew tongue is Abaddon, but in the Greek tongue hath his name Apollyon (Revelation 9:1,3,10-11 KJV).

So when you go to Washington, DC, you can stand at either end of the National Mall and gaze on what is essentially a gigantic talismanic energy-creator. With the domed capitol building at one end and the Washington Monument obelisk at the other, it represents a primeval concept that has only one purpose: regeneration, resurrection, apotheosis—for the incarnation of a deity from the underworld to the earth's surface through the union of these two respective figures, the dome and the obelisk. It doesn't matter whether or not people realize its dark meanings. It does matter that it got built and dedicated that way, and that it is so much like the Vatican.

The U.S. Capitol complex has been called the "mirror Vatican" throughout its history because of the similarities between its primary buildings and streets. It isn't an accident. Do you know what our national forefathers first named the capital city? Instead of Washington, they wanted to name it Rome!

TOO BIG TO IGNORE

When shocking events occur, such as the terrorist attack on the Twin Towers of the World Trade Center and the

Pentagon on September 11, 2001, people are jolted into making new connections. For example, twin towers are symbolic of mysteries within Freemasonry. Initiates in a Masonic Lodge are required to move between two pillars (twin towers) to reach a particular level of knowledge. The pillars represent the earthly and heavenly realms, male and female, active and passive. Some people see an "occult signature" on 9/11.[2] They believe that the magical tradition related to the establishment of a New World Order would require a cataclysmic event, something powerful enough to move beyond the old order of American industrial and financial institutions, a mega "ritual offering" that could facilitate a universal call for bringing order out of chaos and to compel supernatural forces to move the whole nation in new directions. This event would have to be appalling enough to embed itself in everybody's minds to the point where they would be willing to accept a savior—on any terms.

Numerologists say that a foreknowledge of 9/11 had existed for some time. It could be nothing more than a coincidence (and I recognize that all of this is pretty fantastical), but it has to do with folding U.S. paper currency in a certain way. It has been called the "U.S. Currency Origami Prophecy."

Following the attack on the Twin Towers, it was discovered that by folding a new-style (issued since 1998) United States twenty-dollar bill three times in a specific way, you can see what appears to be an image of the Twin Towers hit and smoking, and the Pentagon on fire on the other side. The fact that the folding produces these particular images simultaneously is seen as very significant in occult circles.

After I read about this, I took out new versions of other denominations of currency and folded them in exactly the same way. What I discovered was that if I folded consecutive denominations—that is, a five-dollar bill, a ten-dollar bill, a twenty-dollar bill, a fifty-dollar bill, and a one hundred-dollar bill—and then laid them down in that same order, the pictures created a complete template for the attack. The folded five-dollar bill portrays the Twin Towers standing there unharmed. The folded ten-dollar bill shows the towers after the first airplane strike. The twenty-dollar bill shows the now-iconic image of the two towers smoking, plus the Pentagon smoking on the flip side. Incredibly, the folded fifty-dollar bill shows the towers starting to crumble. And the one hundred-dollar bill depicts the aftermath, with nothing but smoke rising into the air.

Some people consider this proof of a conspiracy theory involving the U.S. government. I look upon it as prophetic evidence of a more insidious nature, one that involves the Masonic history of the founding of the nation and the resulting symbols. As a secret, occult order, Freemasonry has introduced demonic elements into all levels of American government, which means that those elements have infiltrated the DNA of our national identity. This affects military, economic, and moral decisions. It's not just a harmless historical fact and it's not hocus-pocus, either. A strong occult undercurrent links our North American nation with faraway Egypt and ancient biblical warnings.

Demonic elements have infiltrated the DNA of our national identity.

I'm making every effort to keep an eye on Washington in terms of Masonic symbolism and goals. As far as I (and many others) can determine, the Freemasons of the European order (which as many as forty-four of the fifty-six signers of the Declaration of Independence belonged to) were committed to building an occult form of democracy that was based on what's called the Atlantean scheme. They wanted to recreate the mystical kingdom of Atlantis, which they believed had been great because it had taken its order from the gods of ancient history. (This is an extreme condensation of the whole theory, which I have explained more fully in books and interviews.) The tie-in with Freemasonry, especially the highest "degrees" of the order, has got to mean something in terms of the fate of the world. It's just too big to ignore.

GET READY

I write and speak as an American who has studied these things for decades, and who is concerned mostly with how Americans should respond to and be prepared for events and developments in the world.

It is time as never before to sound the alarm, get our act together as Christians, pray, and get ready for the moment when each predicted occurrence suddenly becomes a current, prophecy-fulfilling reality. Pay attention to what's happening, and make sure you keep the words of biblical prophecy in mind as you observe the signs of the times. Prophetically speaking, even Jonathan Edwards, the Great Awakening preacher of the American colonies, had a strong sense that the Antichrist would come on the scene in the decade of the twenty-teens. You can read his predictions in archived letters that he wrote. Prophets around the world and over the centuries have come up with about the same thing, even though most of them had no context for "Christ" so they could not name the evil entity an "Antichrist."

In 2012, the buzz was huge about the so-called Mayan prophecy that said the world was going to end that year. It didn't, obviously. But what people missed in the midst of the sensationalism is the fact that the Mayan calendar never did indicate the end of the world at that point—only the end of an era. That is much more credible, given all of the other prophetic indicators about the rise of an era of unprecedented evil, an era of the final dispensation of humankind, during which a man of great evil will arise unopposed.

Now where does that leave us? There's a lot of scary stuff out there. Should you barricade your doors and adopt a survivalist mentality? Which one of those guys in the news reports is going to be the Antichrist? Who's right? Whom can you believe?

Well, you can believe the words of Jesus, who urged everyone to be ready. Don't be duped into thinking that worldly attainments or world peace are the ultimate goals. Yes, hard times are coming. Jesus said He came to bring, not peace, but a sword (see Matthew 10:34). But you can get through anything if you believe in Him. Make Him your Lord in everything. Don't just "believe" like so many people do, who go to church as a form of fire insurance or who believe in a God-like Santa Claus.

Yes, a better life is possible. It's called eternal life. Don't focus on being able to buy and sell and succeed here, not even if some smooth talker who does not look anything like a beast promises to make you part of an "in" group with guaranteed advancement. Simply stick with old-fashioned repentance. Get right with God now, while there's still time. Start reading your Bible and start worshipping God by doing what He says. All the prophecy in the world cannot tell you when your own personal end is going to come, let alone the end of your world. Put your attention on the eternal life that your Messiah won for you. Then, whatever happens, you will be ready for anything.

ENDNOTES

1. "The Most Approved Plan: the Competition for the Capitol's Design"; Library of Congress website: http://www.loc.gov/exhibits/us.capitol/s2.html; accessed July 7, 2014.

2. For further discussion on how the number 11 is an occult signature, see my book *Zenith 2016* (Crane, MO: Defender, 2013).

Chapter Eight

PRE-TRIBULATION RAPTURE

ANN ROWAN

What does the Bible tell us about the Rapture? What follows in this chapter is the scriptural support for the view that this event (in which dead and living believers in Christ are suddenly caught up to meet the Lord Jesus in the air and to be with Him in heaven) will occur prior to the period of time known as the Tribulation.

Though the term "Rapture" is not in the Bible, Christians being "caught up" or evacuated from the earth is:

> For the Lord himself shall descend from heaven with a shout, with the voice of the archangel, and with the trump of God: and the dead in Christ shall rise first: Then we which are alive and remain shall be caught up together with them in the clouds, to meet the Lord in the air: and so shall we ever be with the Lord (1 Thessalonians 4:16-17 KJV).

This event at Christ's coming will include both living and dead believers. We know that the spirits of dead believers are already in heaven, for the apostle Paul tells us, *"to be absent from the body is to be present with the Lord"* (see 2 Corinthians 5:8). Then, when Jesus comes, the saints' dead bodies will be raised and unified with their spirits at the sound of the trumpet. The living believers' bodies will also be changed, and they will be caught up to meet the Lord in the air. Jesus will not return to earth at that point, but He will take His people to heaven to be with Him. This resurrection will take place instantaneously:

> *Behold! I tell you a mystery. We shall not all sleep, but we shall all be changed, in a moment, in the twinkling of an eye, at the last trumpet. For the trumpet will sound, and the dead will be raised imperishable, and we shall be changed. For this perishable body must put on the imperishable, and this mortal body must put on immortality. When the perishable puts on the imperishable, and the mortal puts on immortality, then shall come to pass the saying that is written: "Death is swallowed up in victory"* (1 Corinthians 15:51-54 ESV).

The mortal bodies that we now have will be changed into bodies that cannot die or corrupt. They will be perfect like Jesus' glorious, resurrected body (see Philippians 3:21). Knowing that He would be returning to heaven soon, Jesus comforted His disciples with the promise of catching away believers to Himself with these words:

> *Let not your heart be troubled: ye believe in God, believe also in me. In my Father's house are many mansions: if it were not so, I would have told you. I go to prepare a place for you. And if I go and prepare a*

place for you, I will come again, and receive you unto
myself; that where I am, there ye may be also (John
14:1-3 KJV).

Here Jesus is very clearly making reference to the traditional Jewish betrothal and wedding ceremony as He
described the reunion of Himself with His Bride, the
Church. The ancient Jewish wedding ceremony foreshad-
ows the Rapture of the Church in many ways. As described
in a previous chapter, during the betrothal period the bride
prepared herself for the bridegroom and the bridegroom
prepared a home for his bride. When the bridegroom had
finished his preparations he would return to the bride's
home to bring her to the wedding. The time of his coming
was a surprise. It was only when the bride heard the loud
celebration of joyous shouts and rams' horns blowing by the
approaching wedding party that she knew the bridegroom
was coming.

Then he would take her to the bridal chamber for the
wedding ceremony and consummation of the marriage. The
wedding feast typically lasted seven days. This foreshad-
ows the seven years that the Church will be hidden in their
heavenly bridal chambers while the inhabitants of the earth
experience God's indignation:

Thy dead men shall live, together with my dead body
shall they arise. Awake and sing, ye that dwell in dust:
for thy dew is as the dew of herbs, and the earth shall
cast out the dead. Come, my people, enter thou into thy
chambers, and shut thy doors about thee: hide thyself as
it were for a little moment, until the indignation be
overpast. For, behold, the Lord cometh out of his place

to punish the inhabitants of the earth for their iniquity: the earth also shall disclose her blood, and shall no more cover her slain (Isaiah 26:19-21 KJV).

THE BLESSED HOPE

For the grace of God that brings salvation hath appeared to all men, teaching us that, denying ungodliness and worldly lusts, we should live soberly, righteously, and godly, in this present world; looking for that blessed hope, and the glorious appearing of the great God and our Savior Jesus Christ (Titus 2:11-13 KJV).

The appearing of the Savior Jesus Christ is a "blessed hope" because He delivers us from the coming wrath. Believers are to look for Jesus' appearing, *not* for God's wrath and judgment, consoling themselves because they know that they will be with the Lord forever.

> *God will save those who are reconciled to Him from the coming time of wrath and judgment of the ungodly.*

If God was willing to send Jesus to the cross for us when we were His enemies, how much more is He willing to save those who are reconciled to Him from the coming time of wrath and judgment of the ungodly? (See Romans 5:8-10.)

THE DAY OF THE LORD

Believers are to *"wait for His Son from heaven, whom He raised from the dead, even Jesus, who delivers us from the wrath to come*" (1 Thessalonians 1:10). Here the Greek word is *apo*, (meaning "from") not *ek* ("out of"). At the Rapture, the Church will be delivered *from* the coming wrath of God, not *out of* the midst of it. God's obedient children will not experience any of God's wrath, for He *"reserves wrath for His enemies"* (Nahum 1:2) and for the *"children of disobedience"* (Colossians 3:6 KJV). That is good news for those who have made Jesus the Lord of their lives, for they will escape the wrath of God. But it's bad news for those who have disobeyed. They will experience the most horrible time that humankind has ever faced on earth.

That time is called the "Great Tribulation" or the "Day of the Lord," as referenced throughout this book. God revealed this coming time of wrath to the ancient Hebrew prophets:

> *For the day of the Lord of hosts shall be upon every one that is proud and lofty, and upon every one that is lifted up; and he shall be brought low* (Isaiah 2:12 KJV).

> *Howl ye; for the day of the Lord is at hand; it shall come as a destruction from the Almighty. Therefore shall all hands be faint, and every man's heart shall melt: And they shall be afraid: pangs and sorrows shall take hold of them; they shall be in pain as a woman that travaileth: they shall be amazed one at another; their faces shall be as flames. Behold, the day of the Lord cometh, cruel both with wrath and fierce anger, to lay the land desolate: and he shall destroy the sinners thereof out of it. For the stars of heaven and the constellations thereof shall not give their light: the sun shall be darkened in his going forth, and the moon*

shall not cause her light to shine. And I will punish the world for their evil, and the wicked for their iniquity; and I will cause the arrogancy of the proud to cease, and will lay low the haughtiness of the terrible (Isaiah 13:6-11 KJV; see also Joel 1:15-20 and Zephaniah 1:14-18).

Woe unto you that desire the day of the Lord! to what end is it for you? the day of the Lord is darkness, and not light. As if a man did flee from a lion, and a bear met him; or went into the house, and leaned his hand on the wall, and a serpent bit him. Shall not the day of the Lord be darkness, and not light? even very dark, and no brightness in it? (Amos 5:18-20 KJV)

We are so used to seeing God as the loving, forgiving God that He is that we sometimes forget that He is also a God of judgment. As the apostle Paul tells us, *"It is a fearful thing to fall into the hands of the living God"* (Hebrews 10:31).

ESCAPING THE WRATH TO COME

Thank God that the Church will not experience God's wrath, because it has been reserved for His enemies: *"For God has not destined us for wrath"* (1 Thessalonians 5:9 ESV).

Scripture clearly states that at the beginning of the seven-year Tribulation period God's wrath will come, and the ungodly will hide in fear:

And the kings of the earth, and the great men, and the rich men, and the chief captains, and the mighty men, and every bondman, and every free man, hid them-selves in the dens and in the rocks of the mountains;

and said to the mountains and rocks, fall on us, and hide us from the face of him that sitteth on the throne, and from the wrath of the Lamb: for the great day of his wrath is come; and who shall be able to stand? (Revelation 6:15-17 KJV)

So we see that God will deliver His people before the day His wrath is poured out upon the earth. Here is a summary:

But of the times and the seasons, brethren, ye have no need that I write unto you. For yourselves know perfectly that the day of the Lord so cometh as a thief in the night. For when they [the unsaved people of the world] *shall say, Peace and safety; then sudden destruction cometh upon them, as travail upon a woman with child; and they shall not escape. But ye, brethren* [Christians], *are not in darkness, that that day should overtake you as a thief. Ye are all the children of light, and the children of the day: we are not of the night, nor of darkness. Therefore let us not sleep, as do others; but let us watch and be sober. For they that sleep sleep in the night; and they that be drunken are drunken in the night. But let us, who are of the day, be sober, putting on the breastplate of faith and love; and for an helmet, the hope of salvation. For God hath not appointed us to wrath but to obtain salvation* [deliverance] *by our Lord Jesus Christ, who died for us, that, whether we wake or sleep, we should live together with him. Wherefore comfort yourselves together, and edify one another...* (1 Thessalonians 5:1-11 KJV).

Those who are saved have the wonderful comfort knowing that they will be delivered by Jesus from wrath. In Luke 21, Jesus describes the Great Tribulation time and then gives a warning and a promise to believers:

> *And take heed to yourselves, lest at any time your hearts be overcharged with surfeiting, and drunkenness, and cares of this life, and so that day come upon you unawares. For as a snare shall it come on all them that dwell on the face of the whole earth. Watch ye therefore, and pray always, that ye may be accounted worthy to escape all these things that shall come to pass, and to stand before the Son of man* (Luke 21:34-36 KJV).

If we watch and pray, staying spiritually alert, we will escape all of the day of the Lord's wrath. In light of all of these wonderful promises, children of God should be looking forward to the Rapture. They can rejoice that they will not be on earth anymore when wickedness is fully unveiled and God's judgment falls:

> *The mystery of lawlessness is already at work. Only he who now restrains it will do so until he is out of the way. And then the lawless one will be revealed, whom the Lord Jesus will kill with the breath of his mouth and bring to nothing by the appearance of his coming* (2 Thessalonians 2:7-8 ESV).

The only force on the earth that is hindering Satan's power is the Church. The Church, the Body of Christ, is the *"he who now restrains."* Only after the Church is caught away will *"the lawless one"* be revealed. God cannot leave His Church on the earth for the seven-year Tribulation time, because He promised that the Church was not appointed for His wrath, but rather to obtain His salvation and deliverance. Second Thessalonians 2:3 states that the Day of the Lord will not come except the *apostasia* comes first. The Amplified Bible Greek scholars note that *apostasia* can accurately be translated as "departure [of the Church]." In other words, the day of the Lord's wrath will not come until the departure (Rapture) occurs first. But once the Church has departed, then the restraining force of the Holy Ghost in the believers will no longer be operating in the earth. With the Church no longer on earth, the Antichrist's power will be able to fully manifest (see 2 Thessalonians 2:9-17).

> *Only after the Church is caught away*
> *will "the lawless one" be revealed.*

Note that the doctrine of the pre-Tribulation Rapture is always characterized as that which brings "good hope" and comfort to the saints. The entire purpose of Paul's letter to the Thessalonians was to assure them that they were not going to go through the time of God's wrath on earth. He wanted to encourage them that they would meet the Lord in the air and be taken to heaven before the Antichrist is revealed. Jesus promised that if we watch and pray always, we can escape *all* (see Luke 21:36) of the Tribulation time of wrath on the earth.

WHEN?

When can we expect this blessed event? No one knows the exact "day and hour," but when we see the signs we can know it is near, right *"at the doors"* (Matthew 24:33).

Hebrews 10:25 lets us know that we can *"see the Day approaching,"* but still, we must never put an exact date on His coming. One undeniable prophetic sign that we are in the latter times (the last days) is that, as of 1948, the Jewish state of Israel has been "born" (established):

> *...In the latter years thou shalt come into the land that is brought back from the sword, and is gathered out of many people, against the mountains of Israel, which have been always waste: but it is brought forth out of the nations, and they shall dwell safely all of them* (Ezekiel 38:8 KJV).

Ezekiel makes reference to the people of Israel being brought back from the sword in the latter years. After the horrors of the World War II Holocaust, the Jewish people were finally given back their homeland in Israel. Psalm 102 gives a prophetic and eerie foreshadowing of the atrocities that the Jewish people endured, but also the promise that God would extend mercy to them. Allusions to distressed prisoners' starvation as well as their bones being burned in the "hearth" (oven) are horribly reminiscent of Hitler's death camps. Verse 16 states that the generation that would see Zion built up (beginning May 14, 1948) would also see the Lord appear in His glory.

Since so much has been fulfilled, prophetically speaking, we can expect the Lord to "appear in His glory" very soon!

Now the Jews have "built up Zion"—they have turned the desert waste places into fruitful places and the "desert is blooming like a rose" (see Isaiah 35:1). Israel has become the breadbasket for that part of the world, producing some of the finest fruits and vegetables through their high-tech agricultural development. Since so much has been fulfilled, prophetically speaking, we can expect the Lord to "appear in his glory" very soon!

Both prophets Joel and Hosea refer to the nation of Israel as a "fig tree." (See Joel 1:7 and Hosea 9:10.) The prophet Jeremiah also refers to the Jewish nation as "figs":

> *One basket had very good figs, even like the figs that are first ripe.... ...Like these good figs, so will I acknowledge them that are carried away captive of Judah, whom I have sent out of this place into the land of the Chaldeans for their good. For I will set mine eyes upon them for good, and I will bring them again to this land: and I will build them, and not pull them down; and I will plant them, and not pluck them up. And I will give them an heart to know me, that I am the Lord: and they shall be my people, and I will be their God...* (Jeremiah 24:2,5-7 KJV).

When Jesus said "behold the fig tree" in the parable of Matthew 24:32-34, He was really saying: "Watch Israel." Before May 14, 1948, it was not possible to "behold the fig tree." But now the fig tree has taken root in her own land and is flourishing. This indicates that we are the generation that will see all of Jesus' prophecies of the end fulfilled. Psalm 102 states that *"the Lord shall build up Zion* [which He has]; *He shall appear in His glory"* (v. 16). The generation that has seen Israel reestablished will see the appearing of Jesus for His Church at the Rapture!

At any time believers can expect Jesus' appearance in the clouds. At that time He will catch them away to heaven—before God's wrath is poured out upon the earth.

RIGHTLY DIVIDE

Confusion arises when some read in the Bible about "the saints" and "the elect" who must endure to the end of the great tribulation; they assume it refers to the Church. They do not recognize that God designates more than one group as His "elect" or "saints." After the Church is raptured, God's focus will be on the nation of Israel. According to Daniel and Jeremiah, there is still the seventieth prophetic "week" (period of seven years) that must be fulfilled, the "time of Jacob's trouble." At that time God will bring about national salvation and deliver Israel.

At the beginning of the Tribulation, the 144,000 elect Jewish "servants of our God" (so designated in Revelation chapter 7) will make Jesus their Messiah—after the Church has departed (see Revelation 7:3-8). Apostle Paul tells us that now, during the church age, *"blindness in part has happened to Israel until the fullness of the Gentiles* [Gentiles saved during the age of grace] *has come in"* (Romans 11:25). When the church age concludes at the Rapture, the Jewish nation's spiritual eyes will be opened and they will receive their Messiah so that *"all Israel will be saved"* (Romans 11:26). We believe that the Church (Jewish and Gentile believers in Messiah) will not go through *any* of the seven-year tribulation time of God's wrath. The "elect" referred to in the book of Revelation and Jesus' Synoptic Gospel prophecies refer to those who receive Jesus after the Rapture.

To rightly interpret the Bible, one must recognize that Jesus' prophecies are directed to different groups at different times.

In order to rightly interpret the Bible, one must recognize that Jesus' prophecies are directed to different groups at different times. Matthew 24 is a classic prophecy chapter in which Jesus addressed four different groups at three different times in history spanning almost two thousand years. Rightly dividing the Word is essential when considering Jesus' end-times prophecies. In His Olivet discourse (Matthew 24), He addressed different prophetic times, starting with the destruction of the Temple in the first century, the signs of the times of our generation that have seen the "fig tree" nation (Israel) reestablished, and the end of the world (the Great Tribulation). Jesus directed His words to three distinct groups: the Church, the 144,000 elect Jewish evangelists, and the Tribulation saints who must *"endure to the end."* Each group was warned of false Christs and false prophets (which is why Jesus repeated the warning three times in one chapter). The Church is warned in Matthew 24 verse 5, the 144,000 elect Jews are warned in verses 10-15, and the Tribulation saints are warned in verses 23 and 24.

Some Jewish believers (Messianic believers) have not properly "divided" Jesus' prophecy. They have assumed that the words directed to the 144,000 male, virgin Jewish evangelists and the Tribulation saints (words about fleeing Jerusalem and admonitions regarding the Sabbath day) are directed to them. However, the Church will already be in heaven before "Jacob's trouble." At the beginning of the Tribulation, the only servants of God on the earth will be the

144,000 Jewish evangelists from the twelve tribes of Israel who will have received Messiah as a result of the preaching of the two witnesses sent from heaven (see Revelation 7:3-8) and who are "sealed" by God. By rightly dividing the Scriptures, we can know who is actually being addressed.

As Second Timothy 3:16 states, *"All Scripture is given by inspiration of God, and is profitable for doctrine, for reproof, for correction, for instruction in righteousness."* Our doctrine cannot be based on a vision, a prophecy, a dream, or any other experience. To get a complete understanding of a doctrine one must take all of the Scripture on a particular topic into consideration (not dismissing any) and keep the Scripture in context. Especially in the case of Bible prophecy, diligent study is required in order to *"rightly divide the word of truth"* (see 2 Timothy 2:15). The context shows which group Jesus is addressing.

MID-TRIBULATION

Let's take a look at this special "elect" group who are raptured in the middle of Jacob's trouble. Daniel 12 describes the mid-Tribulation resurrection of 144,000 sealed, elect Jews:

> *And at that time shall Michael stand up, the great prince which stands for the children of thy people [Daniel, the Jew]: and there shall be a time of trouble, such as never was since there was a nation even to that same time: and at that time thy people shall be delivered, every one that shall be found written in the book. ...And I heard the man clothed in linen, which was upon the waters of the river, when he held up his*

right hand and his left hand unto heaven, and swore by him that lives forever that it shall be for a time, times, and an half; and when he shall have accomplished to scatter the power of the holy people, all these things shall be finished (Daniel 12:1,7 KJV).

This mid-Tribulation Rapture is for the 144,000 Jews and is confirmed in Revelation 14:

Then I looked, and behold, a Lamb standing on [the heavenly] *Mount Zion, and with Him one hundred and forty-four thousand, having His Father's name written on their foreheads. And I heard a voice from heaven, like the voice of many waters, and like the voice of loud thunder. And I heard the sound of harpists playing their harps. They sang as it were a new song before the throne, before the four living creatures, and the elders; and no one could learn that song except the hundred and forty-four thousand who were redeemed from the earth* (Revelation 14:1-3).

WATCH AND BE READY

Christ commands the church to watch and to be ready for His imminent return. He promises if we watch and pray, we can *"escape all these things"* (Luke 21:36). He will deliver the true Church (represented by the church of Philadelphia) from the time of temptation:

Because you have kept My command to persevere, I also will keep you from the hour of trial which shall come upon the whole world, to test those who dwell on the earth. Behold, I am coming quickly! Hold fast what you have, that no one may take your crown (Revelation 3:10-11).

The day and hour of the Rapture is not known, but the exact timing of the Christ's Second Coming can be predicted based on Scripture: *"Immediately after the tribulation of those days"* (Matthew 24:29 ESV), which will be at the end of the seven-year covenant made with the Antichrist. At that time, *"all the tribes of the earth"* will see Him (see Matthew 24:30).

However, at the Rapture Jesus will appear only to *"them that look for him"* (Hebrews 9:28 KJV). At the Rapture, Jesus comes *for* His Church. At the Second Coming, however, the Church will return *with Him,* clothed in fine linen (see Revelation 19:7-8,11-14), to execute judgment upon the nations at the battle of Armageddon (see Jude 14-15; Zechariah 14).

Jesus will come for the Church before the seven-year Tribulation, for the 144,000 in the middle of the seven years, and for the Jews and Tribulation saints when He returns at the end of the seven years.

The book of Revelation is much less confusing once we understand that Jesus will come for the Church *before* the seven-year Tribulation, for the 144,000 in the *middle* of the seven years, and for the Jews and Tribulation saints when He returns at the *end* of the seven years. It can be understood in a chronological and generally literal manner, as the angel Jesus sent to John told him: *"Write the things which thou hast seen, and the things that are, and the things which shall be hereafter"* (Revelation 1:19 KJV). That which he had seen was the glorified Christ (chapter 1); the things *"that are"* refer to the church age (as described in Revelation 2 and 3); and *"hereafter"* refers to after the Church is raptured. The fact that the Church is already in heaven before the judgment seals are loosed in Revelation 6 is confirmed by this passage: *"And round about the throne were four and twenty seats: and upon the seats I saw four and twenty elders sitting, clothed in white raiment; and they had on their heads crowns of gold"* (Revelation 4:4 KJV).

> *At that day believers' crowns will be awarded to the Church when Jesus appears at the Rapture.*

Paul states that we will receive our crowns *"at that day"* and that believers' crowns will be awarded to the Church when Jesus appears at the Rapture: *"Henceforth there is laid up for me a crown of righteousness, which the Lord, the righteous judge, shall give me at that day: and not to me only, but unto all them also that love his appearing"* (2 Timothy 4:8 KJV).

So after the pre-Tribulation Rapture of the Church will come the mid-Tribulation Rapture of the 144,000 elect Jews. The mid-Tribulation Rapture occurs *"when the seventh angel begins to sound,"* right after the two witnesses are resurrected. This is depicted in Revelation 12 by a pregnant woman with twelve stars on her head, the Old Testament symbol for the nation of Israel:

> *Before she travailed, she brought forth; before her pain came, she was delivered of a man child. Who has heard such a thing? Who has seen such things? Shall the earth be made to bring forth in one day? Or shall a nation*

*be born at once? For as soon as Zion travailed, she
brought forth her children* (Isaiah 66:7-8 KJV).

This pregnant woman does *not* refer to the Church.
The Church is the *virgin* Bride who does not complete
her marriage feast to the Lamb until Revelation 19:7 (see
2 Corinthians 11:2; Matthew 25:1). This woman with child
is the nation of Israel. The twelve stars represent the twelve
tribes of Israel (see Genesis 37:9-10). The Satan-inspired
beast (the Antichrist) then invades Israel at the three-and-a-
half year point of the Tribulation (see Daniel 7:24-25; 9:27).
Daniel 11:45 states that when the Antichrist invades Israel
and plants his tabernacle in the holy mountain, then shall
Michael (the archangel) deliver Daniel's people. The timing for the 144,000 Jews to be "delivered" (raptured) is for
a time, times and a half corresponding to Revelation 12:5,
when the offspring of the woman Israel is *"caught up unto
God and His throne."* This "man child" refers to the sealed
Jews who will reign in Jesus' name and authority over the
"nations with a rod of iron."

The mystery is that God's sealed remnant Jews will be
delivered out of the midst of the Tribulation. No other con-
verts during the Tribulation period have that distinction.
After they finish their purpose of evangelizing, the 144,000
Jews will be raptured. Then, the "woman" Israel flees into
the wilderness mountains for safety during the Antichrist
invasion of Jerusalem. The 144,000 elect Jews will already
be in heaven before God's throne, having been *"redeemed
from the earth"* (Revelation 14:3). All of the redeemed Body
of Christ—Jews and Gentiles—will return with Jesus when
He returns to reign on earth at the end of the Tribulation

period. The Bride of Christ in Revelation 19 is depicted in *"fine linen, clean and bright, for the fine linen is the righteous acts of the saints."*

To sum it all up: Those who are watching and ready for Jesus' imminent return will be raptured before the Day of the Lord (also known as the time of Jacob's trouble). The 144,000 sealed Jewish evangelists will be raptured in the middle of the Tribulation time. Those who are converted and endure to the end of the Tribulation (or are martyred) will be raptured/resurrected at the end of the seven years. All three raptures are legitimate and scriptural, and to state that the Church has to endure *any* of God's wrath negates Jesus' promise: *"Watch therefore, and pray always that you may be counted worthy to escape all these things that will come to pass, and to stand before the Son of Man"* (Luke 21:36).

> *Therefore you also be ready, for the Son of Man is coming at an hour you do not expect* (Matthew 24:44).

Chapter Nine

Mid-Tribulation Rapture? I Make My Case

John Shorey

(This chapter is from John Shorey's book, *The Window of the Lord's Return*, available at www.tribulationtruth .com. Used by permission.)

I have organized this chapter in three parts. First, I will cover seven Bible-backed events that must take place in the last generation before the Rapture can occur. Only one of these events (the rebirth of the nation of Israel) has happened to date.

Second, we will study the book of Daniel, which clearly shows that the Rapture will be a mid-Tribulation event.

Third, I will present the teaching from my timeline chart showing a mid-Tribulation Rapture.

Along with the teaching of a pre-Tribulation Rapture has been the teaching of the imminent return of the Lord regarding the Rapture. Many pre-Tribulation Rapture teachers have taught that the timing of the Rapture has been imminent for almost two thousand years! I was discussing this point with one pastor friend and told him, "How could the Rapture have been imminent for even one hundred years if Israel had not been reborn as a nation until 1948?" His response was, "Well, now it is imminent." To counter my friend's response I will show six more events from Scripture that must take place before the Rapture.

PART ONE
THE REMAINING SIX EVENTS THAT MUST OCCUR BEFORE THE RAPTURE

There was one verse that convinced me that the Rapture was not an imminent event. After more than three years of working on this study, I believe, with the help of the Holy Spirit, I now see that from the time of the rebirth of Israel in 1948 (the event that triggers the beginning of the last generation before the return of the Lord Jesus), there are at least six more events that must happen before the Rapture of the believers.

1. *The one-world government must be in place before the Rapture can occur.*

God's Word indicates that before the Antichrist can be revealed, the ten leaders, or as I call them, "the ten heads of state," and the one-world government must be in place. Many surmise that the future one-world government will be comprised of ten regions of the world, with a leader over each region. This would correspond to the "ten horns" in the book of Revelation.

Now if we draw from the generally accepted teaching of the coming Antichrist, you will see most prophetic teachers say that the man who will become the Antichrist will already be the leader of the one-world government. This leader will be mortally wounded and then his miraculous recovery will usher in his emergence as the Antichrist. Now go back and read Revelation 13:3 (NIV): *"One of the heads of the beast seemed to have had a fatal wound, but the fatal wound had been healed."* This verse does not say the overall leader of this one-world government will be wounded. No! It says *one* of the heads of this government will be wounded. This means to qualify as a candidate for the Antichrist, the person must be one of the ten heads, not the overall leader.

Why is this an important distinction? Because even as a one-world government is created and a leader is established, we will still not know the identity of the Antichrist. This will be revealed when one of the ten heads of state is fatally wounded, and then the wound is healed as he is possessed by Satan.

Since Second Thessalonians 2:1-3 says the gathering of believers, or the Rapture, cannot occur until the Antichrist is revealed, and the Antichrist cannot be revealed until the one-world government is in place first, we can conclude that the one-world government must precede the Rapture. By connecting this fact to the second event listed on my timeline (see pages 166-167) that shows a great falling away, we then begin to see a sequence of events that must come together before the Rapture.

2. *There must be a falling away.*

Events two and three are connected and are explained in the following sections.

3. The Antichrist must be revealed.

As you read the following events that must happen before the Rapture can occur, you realize this is not my opinion; this is the Word of God.

> Concerning the coming of our Lord Jesus Christ and our being gathered to him, we ask you, brothers and sisters, not to become easily unsettled or alarmed by the teaching allegedly from us—whether by prophecy or by word of mouth or by letter—asserting that the day of the Lord has already come. Don't let anyone deceive you in any way, for that day will not come until the rebellion occurs and the man of lawlessness is revealed, the man doomed to destruction (2 Thessalonians 2:1-3 NIV).

These verses are talking about the man of lawlessness, the son of perdition, or the Antichrist, who must come before the day of the Lord or the Rapture can occur. These verses also talk about the rebellion; this is referred to in other translations as a great "falling away." When I discuss my timeline chart, I will go into more detail as to why we will be set up for a great falling away before the coming Antichrist even arrives. Some sort of global crisis is coming; this event must happen to convince the world that the solution to these global problems is a global currency and one-world government. When this crisis arrives, the United States of America will experience a total breakdown of society as we know it. Many Christians will believe the Great Tribulation has already started. Many Christians will realize that they were not taught correctly concerning the Rapture; and I believe this will lead large numbers of Christians to leave their faith, causing a great "falling away."

4. The Temple must be rebuilt before the Rapture can occur.

This event is explained with event number five.

5. The Antichrist must desecrate the Temple before the Rapture can occur.

The following Scriptures show that both the Temple must be rebuilt and the Antichrist must desecrate the Temple before the prophecy of these verses can come to pass. The Bible covers both of these events together.

Mark 13:14,26-27 (NIV) says, *"When you see 'the abomination that causes desolation' standing where it does not belong—let the reader understand—then let those who are in Judea flee to the mountains. ...At that time people will see the Son of Man coming in the clouds with great power and glory. And he will send his angels and gather his elect from the four winds, from the ends of the earth to the ends of the heavens."* This passage refers to the Antichrist standing in the Temple in verse 14; then verse 27 shows the Rapture following this event.

To give a second witness to God's own words, let's read Matthew 24:15,30 (NIV):

> So when you see standing in the holy place "the abomination that causes desolation," spoken of through the prophet Daniel—let the reader understand.... Then will appear the sign of the Son of Man in heaven. And then all the peoples of the earth will mourn when they see the Son of Man coming on the clouds of heaven, with power and great glory."

These verses show that the Rapture cannot happen until the Temple is rebuilt because how can the Antichrist stand in a Temple and desecrate a Temple that has not yet been rebuilt? *Matthew 24:30 shows the Rapture happening after the desecration of the Temple.* If you look up Daniel 9:27, you will see the timing of this desecration of the Temple.

6. Heavenly events must also take place before the Rapture occurs.

This is another instance where it is best to let God's Word speak for itself:

> *Immediately after the distress of those days "the sun will be darkened, and the moon will not give its light; the stars will fall from the sky, and the heavenly bodies will be shaken." **Then** will appear the sign of the Son of Man in heaven. **And then** all the peoples of the earth will mourn when they see the Son of Man coming on the clouds of heaven, with power and great glory. And he will send his angels with a loud trumpet call, and they will gather his elect from the four winds, from one end of the heavens to the other* (Matthew 24:29-31 NIV).

Next, read Revelation 6:12-13 (NIV):

> *I watched as he opened the sixth seal. There was a great earthquake. The sun turned black like sackcloth made of goat hair, the whole moon turned blood red, and the stars in the sky fell to the earth, as figs drop from a fig tree when shaken by a strong wind.*

As you read these verses, notice they both refer to the stars falling from the sky. These would be meteor showers. The reference in Revelation 6 places this event at the sixth seal, and the reference from Matthew 24 shows the Rapture happening after this event. (Note: In addition to a total lunar eclipse, blood moon events have been explained by science to occur from the atmospheric dust caused by forest fires and volcanic eruptions.)

Notice all six of these last remaining events occur during a time period that is recognized as happening during the Great Tribulation. When these events that I have just outlined come to pass, it will be the time for us to stand up and look up as God has told us in Luke 21:28 (NIV): *"When these things begin to take place, stand up and lift up your heads, because your redemption is drawing near."*

Truly, the last thing that will happen before the Lord returns will be the blowing of the trumpet, or the "last trumpet" as it is referred to in First Corinthians 15:51-52 (NIV): *"We will all be changed—in a flash, in the twinkling of an eye, at the **last trumpet**. For the trumpet will sound, the dead will be raised imperishable, and we will be changed."*

PART TWO
TIMING OF THE RAPTURE FROM THE BOOK OF DANIEL

Upon much study, I have found more evidence that the Rapture does not happen until the middle of the Great Tribulation. In the first half of Daniel 7, we have the vision of Daniel described and then explained in the second half. I will show parallel links in the New Testament that refer to the same events. I conclude by showing you that Daniel's vision not only contains information on the Antichrist's war against the saints, but it also shows the deliverance of the saints in the Rapture. Then I will take you on a further study of Daniel that shows beyond all doubt that the Rapture will be a mid-Tribulation event.

Please maintain an open mind as you proceed in this study. It is hard for many people to believe as they have never seen what I am showing plainly written in God's Word.

First, let us read the end of Daniel's vision found in Daniel 7:13-14 (NIV):

> *In my vision at night I looked, and there before me was one like a son of man, coming with the clouds of heaven. He approached the Ancient of Days and was led into his presence. He was given authority, glory, and sovereign power; all nations and peoples of every language worshiped him. His dominion is an everlasting dominion that will not pass away, and his kingdom is one that will never be destroyed.*

When we read this, we recognize that Jesus is the One who is coming in the clouds. Jesus is coming in the clouds to deliver the saints from the persecution of the Antichrist and to take them to His Father's kingdom. Looking further at this verse, you will see it is addressing the Gentiles, not the Jews, as this event is the Rapture of the saints out of all nations of the world.

Daniel 7:14 (NIV) says, *"He was given authority, glory and sovereign power; all nations and peoples of every language worshiped him."* My point will become even clearer as the meaning of Daniel's visions and dreams are explained in the second half of Daniel 7.

Read Daniel 7:21-22 (NIV): *"As I watched, this horn was waging war against the holy people* [saints] *and defeating them, until the Ancient of Days came and pronounced judgment in favor of the holy people* [saints] *of the Most High, and the time came when they possessed the kingdom."*

I believe *"kingdom"* is referring to the kingdom of heaven. For the saints, to possess the kingdom of heaven, they have to go to heaven.

> **For the saints, to possess the kingdom of heaven, they have to go to heaven.**

Now let's look at the parallel of Jesus coming in the clouds for His saints from Matthew 24:29-31 (NIV 1984):

> *Immediately after the distress of those days, "the sun will be darkened, and the moon will not give its light; the stars will fall from the sky, and the heavenly bodies will be shaken." At that time the sign of the Son of Man will appear in the sky. And then all the nations of the earth will mourn. They will see the Son of Man coming on the clouds of the sky, with power and great glory. And he will send his angels with a loud trumpet call, and they will gather his elect from the four winds, from one end of the heavens to the other.*

These verses from Matthew are almost verbatim as those in Mark 13:24-27 and Acts 2:20 (NIV): *"The sun will be turned to darkness and the moon to blood before the coming of the great and glorious day of the Lord."* These events are also seen in Revelation 6 with the opening of the seals. Notice the fifth seal is the martyrdom of the saints, parallel to what is happening in Daniel and described as war on the saints.

Please stay with me, for it is about to get very interesting; for now I will further link these Scriptures to the books of Revelation and Acts. Let's read again Revelation 6:12-13 (NIV):

> *I watched as he opened the sixth seal. There was a great earthquake. The sun turned black like sackcloth made of goat hair, the whole moon turned blood red, and the stars in the sky fell to the earth, as figs drop from a fig tree when shaken by a strong wind.*

What is spoken of in Revelation 6:12-13 is the fulfillment of that which Acts 2:20 says must happen before the day of the Lord comes. Acts 2:20 (NIV) says, *"The sun will be turned into darkness and the moon to blood before the coming of the great and glorious day of the Lord."* Some may ask, "Is the Rapture the day of the Lord?" Second Peter 3:10 (NIV) throws light on this question, *"But the day of the Lord will come like a thief."*

I will show you the arrival of the saints in heaven as described in Daniel 7:13 and Revelation 7:9.

First, read Daniel 7:13-14 (NIV): *"In my vision at night I looked, and there before me was one like a son of man, coming with the clouds of heaven. He approached the Ancient of Days and was led into his presence. He was given authority, glory and sovereign power; all nations and peoples of every language worshiped him...."*

Now read Revelation 7:9 (NIV): *"After this I looked, and there before me was a great multitude that no one could count, from every nation, tribe, people, and language, standing before the throne and before the Lamb. They were wearing white robes and were holding palm branches in their hands."*

To bring these thoughts to their conclusion, I want to share the meaning of Daniel's vision that was given to him in the second half of Daniel 7. First, I want to show the verse in Daniel that describes the Antichrist waging war against the saints until God steps in and delivers them. This deliverance is the Rapture that is described as the Son of Man coming in the clouds in Daniel 7:13. It is shown in greater detail in Matthew 24:29-31. Next, read Daniel 7:21-22 (NIV):

> *As I watched, this horn was waging war against the holy people* [saints] *and defeating them, until the Ancient of Days came and pronounced judgment in favor of the holy people* [saints] *of the Most High, and the time came when they possessed the kingdom.*

What is interesting is this oppression or war against the saints has an ending point described in this verse. It says the horn is waging war against the saints and defeating them until the Ancient of Days steps in to deliver them.

In reading the next verse, you will see how long the saints must endure oppression from the Antichrist: *"He will speak against the Most High and oppress his holy people* [saints] *and try to change the set times and the laws. The holy people* [saints] *will be delivered into his hands for a time, times and half a time"* (Daniel 7:25 NIV). The note in the margin of my Thompson Study Bible says this time is three and one-half years. Think about this. The Antichrist appears on the scene at the opening of the first seal of Revelation 6. The Antichrist is not on the earth as the actual Antichrist until Satan possesses one of the horns or heads of the beast and brings this head of state back from the dead. Once Satan is this world leader in human form, you can be sure he will lash out against the saints almost immediately.

Daniel teaches that the Antichrist will broker a seven-year peace with Israel soon after he comes to power. The Bible supports that this is the beginning of the seven-year Great Tribulation. What is interesting is the Antichrist will only be able to make war against the saints for three and one-half years, according to Daniel 7:25. Why will the Antichrist no longer be able to make war on the saints? Daniel 7:21-22 reveals the reason: God intervenes! What is the form of this intervention? Jesus is coming in the clouds and raptures the saints! Put these thoughts all together, and you have the Rapture occurring three and one-half years into the Great Tribulation.

God intervenes!

This part of my study is very compelling, showing a period of three and a half years of war on the saints, followed by our heavenly Father's intervention. What I will show you now is a parallel Scripture passage from Revelation 13 that confirms this three-and-one-half-year period, which will end at God's intervention with the Rapture of the saints.

> *The beast was given a mouth to utter proud words and blasphemies and to exercise its authority for forty-two months. It opened its mouth to blaspheme God, and to slander his name and his dwelling place and those who live in heaven. It was given power to wage war*

against God's holy people [saints] *and to conquer them. And it was given authority over every tribe, people, language and nation* (Revelation 13:5-7 NIV).

Notice, this passage says the beast, the Antichrist, was given authority for forty-two months. Some have taken this to mean that the Antichrist would only appear on the scene for forty-two months. This does not make sense because the Antichrist makes a seven-year peace with Israel and breaks it in the middle. This passage is saying the same thing as what Daniel chapter 7 is saying. The Antichrist has been given authority over the saints for forty-two months, and after that period, just as Daniel 7:21-22 says, God intervenes: *"As I watched, this horn was waging war against the holy people* [saints] *and defeating them, until the Ancient of Days came and pronounced judgment in favor of the holy people* [saints] *of the Most High, and the time came when they possessed the kingdom."*

I believe I have shown a strong case for the Rapture as a mid-Tribulation event from the book of Daniel. Now I offer further biblical support from the book of Daniel that shows the Rapture as a mid-Tribulation event.

If you read Daniel 12:1-2, you will realize these verses are talking about the time of the Great Tribulation. These verses then describe a deliverance from this time of Great Tribulation. (Notice that Michael the archangel is standing up and ready to play a part in this coming deliverance.) What is the form of this deliverance? If you notice who is included in this event, you will realize it must be talking about the Rapture of the saints.

At that time Michael, the great prince who protects your people, will arise. There will be a time of

> *distress such as has not happened from the begin-*
> *ning of nations until then. But at that time your*
> *people—everyone whose name is found written in*
> *the book—will be delivered. Multitudes who sleep*
> *in the dust of the earth will awake: some to everlast-*
> *ing life, others to shame and everlasting contempt*
> (Daniel 12:1-2 NIV).

When you see the dead in Christ who have their names written in the Book of Life awakening from the sleep of death, clearly the event described here is the Rapture.

First Thessalonians 4:15-18 (NIV) says:

> *According to the Lord's word, we tell you that we*
> *who are still alive, who are left until the coming of*
> *the Lord, will certainly not precede those who have*
> *fallen asleep. For the Lord himself will come down*
> *from heaven, with a loud command, with the voice of*
> *the archangel and with the trumpet call of God, and*
> *the dead in Christ will rise first. After that, we who*
> *are still alive and are left will be caught up with them*
> *in the clouds to meet the Lord in the air. And so we*
> *will be with the Lord forever. Therefore encourage one*
> *another with these words.*

This is a WOW moment for me. *"For the Lord himself will come down from heaven, with a loud command, with the voice of the archangel...."* Michael is the archangel, one of the top generals in command of the armies of God, and Daniel 12:1 shows Michael getting ready to play his part in the Rapture of all those whose names are written in the Book of Life, who are the elect of God—the saints.

It is interesting that after these coming events were described in Daniel 12:1-2, it goes on to say in Daniel 12:4 that these words were to be sealed up until the time of the end, *"But you, Daniel, roll up and seal the words of the scroll until the time of the end."* Reading further, it gets very interesting as verses 5-7 describe two men standing on both sides of the river talking to a man in linen who was above them. I believe the man in linen was Jesus and the other two may have been Michael the archangel (and maybe another angel). One of the men or an angel asks the question, *"How long will it be before these astonishing things are fulfilled?"* What are the *"astonishing things"*? The things referred to in Daniel 12:1-2 are the time of the Great Tribulation up until the time of the deliverance of God's people whose names are written in the Book of Life, both the living and those who are dead in the Lord. Then the man in linen—whom I believe is Jesus—answers the question and describes this time as *a time, times and half a time* (or three and one-half years). This places the Rapture three and one-half years into the Great Tribulation.

God Himself will come down from heaven...

Now read Daniel 12:5-7 and see if what I am saying makes sense:

> *Then I Daniel, looked, and there before me stood two others, one on this bank of the river and one on the opposite bank. One of them said to the man clothed in linen, who was above the waters of the river, "How long will it be before these astonishing things are fulfilled?" The man clothed in linen who was above*

the waters of the river, lifted his right hand and his left hand toward heaven, and I heard him swear by him who lives forever, saying, "It will be for a time, times and half a time. When the power of the holy people has been finally broken, all these things will be completed."

Again, notice the last part of the answer from the man in linen. It says that once the power of the holy people has been broken, all these things will be completed. Realize that during this time of the Great Tribulation, the Antichrist has been waging war against the saints. About this time, the Antichrist will enter the Temple and declare that he is God.

Now get the picture of what is happening here. Daniel just had it explained to him how long it would be until these astonishing things would be fulfilled. However, Daniel still does not get the full picture. So again, he asks another question. The question is not about the fulfillment of the astonishing things but about the outcome of all of these things.

I heard, but I did not understand. So I asked, "My lord, what will the outcome of all this be?" He replied, "Go your way, Daniel, because the words are closed up and sealed until the time of the end. Many will be purified, made spotless and refined, but the wicked will continue to be wicked. None of the wicked will understand, but those who are wise will understand. From the time that the daily sacrifice is abolished and the abomination that causes desolation is set up, there will be 1,290 days (Daniel 12:8-11 NIV).

This is another revelation moment for me. Daniel has had two questions answered in Daniel 12. The first question concerned the time when the astonishing things would be fulfilled. He was told it would be three and one-half years until the time that the saints would be delivered, coinciding with the Antichrist desecrating the Temple. Then Daniel asked what the outcome of all this would be. The King James Version says Daniel asked, *"What shall be the end of these things?"* He was told it will be three and one-half years from the time the daily sacrifice is abolished, the same time that the Antichrist is desecrating the Temple, until all these things will come to their end.

The answers to these two questions have established two things: how long from the beginning of the Great Tribulation to the deliverance of the saints (three and one-half years) and how long from the desecration of the Temple until the end of these things, again three and one-half years. I believe God's Word in Daniel 12 supports my conclusion that the Rapture of the Church occurs in the middle of the seven-year Great Tribulation period.

Is it really that important when the Lord returns? Should not we just be ready?

In closing Part Two, consider the questions that some will ask, "Is it really that important when the Lord returns? Should not we just be ready?" These are two good questions. If the Church has been taught that the Rapture will come before the Great Tribulation starts, this gives the Church a false sense of security. I have heard pastors say God would not allow His Church to go through suffering.

Revelation 14:11-13 shows that the saints will have to have patient endurance during the Great Tribulation. This will also be the time when the Antichrist is pushing his system of the mark of the beast.

If the saints who have expected the pre-Tribulation Rapture suddenly realize they are in the Great Tribulation with no warning to prepare for this turbulent time, I believe it will cause many Christians to turn away from God. Some will believe God has abandoned them and that their Christian leaders have misled them. They will then accept the system of the Antichrist, rather than starve to death. I believe the events happening today with the world economies on the verge of collapse are setting the stage to make it easy for the world populations to accept a savior in the form of the Antichrist.

We, as believers, have to be the ones looking for the signs of Christ's coming. I am convinced we must prepare for hard times as Joseph did, so when the hard times come, we will be able to take care of the needs of our families and others. We need to be in a position for God to use us for the greatest revival the world has ever seen! If what I have written in this chapter makes sense, I urge you to shout it from the housetops and help spread the message, for the time is short.

PART THREE
TIMELINE* OF EVENTS LEADING
TO THE RAPTURE

TIMELINE OF EVENTS

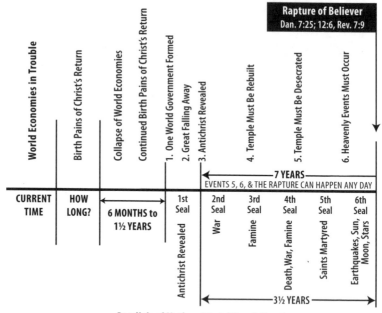

Parallels of Mathew 24 and Revelation 6

*Timeline from *The Window of the Lord's Return* by John Shorey; available at www.tribulationtruth.com.

This timeline of events has what I call three layers, like a three layer cake, that brings us to the same conclusion: the Rapture is a mid-Tribulation event. Then I conclude with what I call the "icing on the cake."

The first layer covers the six remaining events discussed earlier in this chapter, which the Bible shows must happen before the Rapture can occur. A seventh event that precedes the Rapture—the rebirth of Israel in 1948—has already occurred.

The second layer of the timeline covers the seven seals. I will initially cover only the first six seals as this will show how this layer intersects with the first layer of my teaching.

LEADING TO THE RAPTURE

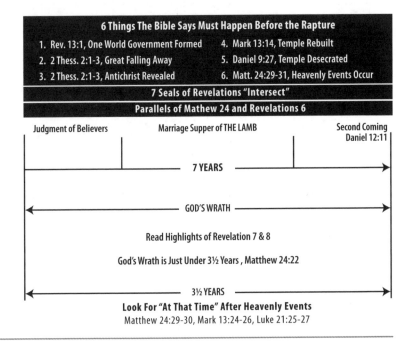

The third layer covers the parallels between Matthew 24 and other Gospel accounts with Revelation 6 and the seven seals of Revelation.

You will have to wait until the end to see what the "icing on the cake" covers.

My timeline chart starts with our current situation—global economies are in trouble. A collapse could start in Europe and domino to the U.S., or it could start in America and domino to Europe. The truth is the economies of the world are now all tied together. The timing of a collapse is a question mark on my timeline chart. Global economies are so fragile; things could literally fall apart tomorrow. I believe all that is keeping this from happening is the timing of God.

Once an economic collapse happens, within days, life as we know it in America will be over. We will see panic buying of food. Credit cards will no longer work, and what real money you have will have little to no value. We will see riots, anarchy, and the institution of martial law. Many Christians will believe the Great Tribulation has begun. The truth is the Great Tribulation cannot start until the Antichrist comes to power, and that cannot happen until a global one-world government is fully in place. It could take from six months to a year or more before America will give up its Constitution, Bill of Rights, freedom of speech, freedom of religion, and the right to bear arms, and join the one-world government.

During this time, I believe it will be the greatest opportunity the world has ever seen to witness to the lost. But if we don't see these events coming and get prepared for this time, we won't be able to help our lost friends and family. How can we help minister to the lost if we are basket cases ourselves? Remember, God warned Joseph in Egypt, and his preparation saved his family.

As you study my timeline at the beginning of this section, you will see the first layer was covered earlier in this chapter under the six remaining things the Bible says must happen before the Rapture. The next layer is the seven seals of the book of Revelation 6. The sixth event in my first layer and the 6th seal of Revelation 6 are the same event. The heavenly events from the first layer come from the book of Matthew and the other Gospels, and the heavenly events in the second layer come from the sixth seal of Revelation 6, thus showing the first two layers intersect at this point.

The third layer of my timeline draws parallels between Matthew 24 and the other Gospels, and the opening of the seals in Revelation 6. If you study Matthew 24 and Revelation 6, you will recognize that these two books are covering the same events. Matthew 24 contains almost a complete outline for the seals covered in Revelation 6.

If you will read each of the three Gospel references I show on the third layer of my chart, you will see that each reference shows the sun goes black and then it says, *"**At that time** the sign of the Son of Man will appear in the sky."*

> *Immediately after the distress of those days, "the sun will be darkened, and the moon will not give its light; the stars will fall from the sky, and heavenly bodies will be shaken." **At that time** the sign of the Son of Man will appear in the sky and all the nations of the earth will mourn. They will see the Son of Man coming on the clouds of the sky with power and great glory. And he will send his angels with a loud trumpet call, and they will gather his elect from the four winds, from one end of the heavens to the other* (Matthew 24:29-31 NIV 1984).

As revealed previously, three Gospel references show the sun goes black and the moon will not give its light. Read Matthew 24:29-31 and then read Mark 13:24-26 and Luke 21:25-27. Notice the same sequence of events. The sun goes black and the moon will not give its light. Next it says, *"At that time the sign of the Son of Man will appear in the sky...."*

Now we need to read about the sixth seal in the book of Revelation and see how it progresses to the Rapture. Revelation 6:12-13 says: *"I watched as he opened the sixth seal. There was a great earthquake. The sun turned black like sackcloth made of goat hair, the whole moon turned blood red, and the stars in the sky fell to earth, as late figs drop from a fig tree when shaken by a strong wind."*

If I am making a good case for the Rapture happening after the opening of the sixth seal, then what I want to propose is that the opening of the seventh seal is the Rapture.

Revelation 8:1 says, *"When he opened the seventh seal, there was silence in heaven for about half an hour."* I believe when we arrive in heaven at the time of the Rapture, we will be in awe and all the heavenly beings will be in awe to see the plan of God's redemption unfolding at the throne of God. All will be silent (a holy hush, if you will) until our heavenly Father breaks the silence and welcomes us, the Bride of His Son Jesus, to our new home.

In Revelation 7, we see the arrival of the saints at the seventh seal:

> *After this I looked, and there before me was a great multitude that no one could count, from every nation, tribe, people and language, standing before the throne and before the Lamb. They were wearing white robes and were holding palm branches in their hands* (Revelation 7:9 NIV).

Then one of the elders who is always at the throne of God speaks. Revelation 7:13-14 (NIV) says:

Then one of the elders asked me, "These in white robes—who are they, and where did they come from?" I answered, "Sir, you know." And he said, "These are they who have come out of the great tribulation; they have washed their robes and made them white in the blood of the Lamb."

When we go back to the opening of the seventh seal, you will see after all the saints are safe at our heavenly Father's throne, the seven angels are given the seven trumpets and released to deliver the wrath of God to an unrepentant world. Revelation 8:1-2 (NIV) says, *"When he opened the seventh seal, there was silence in heaven for about half an hour. And I saw the seven angels who stand before God, and seven trumpets were given to them."*

If you will take the time to look up the other Bible verses listed on my chart, I believe you will see the full picture of the Rapture unfold that I have described here.

The icing on the cake!

Now for the "icing on the cake." A proper title would be, "Darkness Comes before Deliverance." As I already pointed out, there are three separate accounts in the Gospels showing that when the sun goes dark, *"At that time the sign of the Son of Man will appear in the clouds."* When the sun goes dark, we can truly look up, for our redemption draws near.

If we turn to the book of Exodus, we see the account of Moses getting ready to lead God's people to freedom. The last plague before the plague of the firstborn was darkness. Exodus 10:21 (NIV) says, *"Then the Lord said to Moses,*

'Stretch out your hand toward the sky so that darkness will spread over Egypt, darkness that can be felt.'" When Moses did as God instructed, it was dark for three days. This was the last plague before deliverance. Following the darkness was the plague of the firstborn. This event was deliverance for God's children who were under the blood. But it was judgment for those who were not under the blood.

Just before Jesus died on the cross, it was dark for three hours. Mark 15:33 (NIV) says, *"At noon, darkness came over the whole land until three in the afternoon."* Then we read a further account of the crucifixion found in John 19:30 (NIV): *"When he had received the drink, Jesus said, 'It is finished.' With that, he bowed his head and gave up his spirit."* At the crucifixion, it was dark for three hours before Jesus died, and we were delivered from sin.

Next are the events at the end of the sixth seal as shown in Matthew 24:29-31 (NIV 1984):

> *Immediately after the distress of those days, the sun will be darkened and the moon will not give its light: the stars will fall from the sky, and the heavenly bodies will be shaken. At that time the sign of the son of man will appear in the sky, and all the nations of the earth will mourn. They will see the Son of Man coming on the clouds of the sky, with power and great glory. And he will send his angels with a loud trumpet call, and they will gather his elect from the four winds, from one end of the heavens to the other.*

What does "At that time" mean? It's obvious to me. It means when the sun goes black and the moon does not give its light. "At that time" is the Rapture.

I will share one last verse from the Old Testament showing the Rapture after the darkness, Joel 2:30-31 (NIV):

> *I will show wonders in the heavens and on the earth, blood and fire and billows of smoke. The sun will be turned to darkness and the moon to blood before the coming of the great and dreadful day of the Lord.*

There are three key points to look at in these verses. Points one and two are from the verse that says *the great and dreadful day.* It will be great for God's people and dreadful for the unrepentant. Go back to the sixth seal of Revelation 6 where it says, *"The sun turned black like sackcloth made of goat hair."* This is the part of the sixth seal that causes us, the redeemed, to rejoice. When you read a bit further, you will see where it is a dreadful day for the unrepentant.

> *The heavens receded like a scroll being rolled up, and every mountain and island was removed from its place. Then the kings of the earth, the princes, the generals, the rich, the mighty, and everyone else, both slave and free, hid in caves and among the rocks of the mountains. They called to the mountains and the rocks, "Fall on us and hide us from the face of him who sits on the throne and from the wrath of the Lamb! For the great day of their wrath has come, and who can withstand it?"* (Revelation 6:14-17 NIV)

This excites me. We have just been delivered from harm's way, the war on the saints is over, and we are about to be welcomed by our heavenly Father as Jesus leads His Bride to the throne to meet Him.

The last point of interest in the verse in Joel 2:30-31 is the phrase, "Day of the Lord," often referenced in the Bible as the time of the Rapture.

I have made my case. Now I ask you, the reader, to examine the Scriptures to see if what I am presenting is sound.

Chapter Ten

ARE YOU READY FOR THE GREAT TRIBULATION?

RON CANTOR

Arrogance is unbecoming even when you can back it up. But it is particularly ugly when you can't! When it comes to eschatology, the study of the end times, it is important that we maintain an attitude of humility. No one can be 100 percent sure they are right. John the Baptist doubted Yeshua (see Matthew 11); the disciples expected Israel's full restoration immediately after He arose (see Acts 1:6), something that will happen in the Father's time (see Acts 1:7); Peter rebuked the Son of God for foretelling His death (see Mark 8:31-32); and many believers in the first century were quite sure the Lord would return in their lifetime.

As we address the subject of the timing of the Rapture, I have no desire to come across as a know-it-all. I am not a scholar—just a guy who reads the Bible. But I don't believe that the Bible was written in a way that only scholars could interpret it. This is why the Catholic Church in the Middle Ages only allowed a select few to be entrusted with the Scriptures—they did not want lay people, and even many priests, to read the Bible for themselves. In Judaism, most rely on the interpretations of the sages and rabbis before them. But God wants us *to think for ourselves.*

I recognize that there are many people who hold to a pre-Tribulation view of the Rapture who are humble and knowledgeable. I also recognize that my view is not the only valid view. I only ask that you consider the thoughts presented in this chapter with an open heart.

Consider the thoughts presented with an open heart.

It has come as a surprise to me though, that many in the pre-Tribulation camp can look at those with a different theology as if they are heretics. They act as if the pre-Tribulation view is time-honored doctrine, as opposed to an idea that is not even 200 years old. While teaching in a Bible school years ago, I was encouraged to hide my views on the end times. It was not as if I had doubts regarding the divinity of Yeshua. Disagreement over end-times prophecy is not an issue that should divide us. Should we talk about it? Absolutely—but we should maintain mutual respect and humility toward each other.

RAPTURE

The word "rapture" means to be *caught up.* The Bible clearly teaches that at the end of the age believers will be caught up in the sky to meet Yeshua and spend eternity with Him. Concerning this truth, there is little disagreement. This is the great and awesome hope of the Bride of Messiah. Yeshua promised that He would return for her (see John 14:3).

The most common passage that refers to believers being caught up or raptured is First Thessalonians 4:16-17 (NIV):

> *For the Lord himself will come down from heaven, with a loud command, with the voice of the archangel and with the trumpet call of God, and the dead in Christ* [Messiah] *will rise first. After that, we who are still alive and are left will be caught up together with them in the clouds to meet the Lord in the air. And so we will be with the Lord forever.*

Once again, there is very little controversy about whether or not there will be a Rapture. The controversy is concerning the *timing* of the Rapture—when will it happen? There are three basic views:

1. Pre-Tribulation: We are raptured before the Great Tribulation.[1]

2. Mid-Tribulation: After the first three and one-half years of the reign of the Antichrist, just as he begins to show his true colors and instigates massive persecution against the Jews, the Church will be raptured.

3. Post-Tribulation or Pre-Wrath: The wrath of God is poured out on the wicked at the end of the Great Tribulation. Believers go through the Great Tribulation, but enjoy God's protection (like Israel in Goshen). Just before God judges the wicked, He removes the righteous (as in the case of Lot and Sodom and Gomorrah) by means of the Rapture. We meet Yeshua in

the clouds and return with Him to judge the nations.

Of course only one of these can be correct. It is not like we get raptured according to our theology!

For a long time I was not concerned over which view people held. As I stated, minor doctrinal issues should not divide the body of believers. And I still believe that this should not divide us, but I don't see this any longer as a *minor* issue. I came to the conclusion many years ago that this was not some secondary back-burner issue, but something that believers need to take very seriously. Why?

SUFFERING

Let us just suppose that view number three, post-Tribulation, or pre-Wrath as some now call it, is the correct view. What will happen to all those who were expecting to be raptured before the Tribulation—*before* the suffering and persecution begins? My deep concern is for those who are not ready—those who are assuming they will never suffer. We often hear preachers warn believers to be ready to be raptured at any time. But rarely do we hear them warn people to be ready to endure. The emphasis in the book of Revelation, the most significant book on the end times, is not on the Rapture! The theme of revelation is *endure to the end!*

> *You have persevered and have endured hardships for my name, and have not grown weary* (Revelation 2:3 NIV).

> *Since you have kept my command to endure patiently, I will also keep you from the hour of trial that is going*

to come on the whole world to test the inhabitants of the earth (Revelation 3:10 NIV).

I, John, your brother and companion in the suffering and kingdom and patient endurance that are ours in Jesus, was on the island of Patmos because of the word of God and the testimony of Jesus (Revelation 1:9 NIV).

Do not be afraid of what you are about to suffer. I tell you, the devil will put some of you in prison to test you, and you will suffer persecution for ten days. Be faithful, even to the point of death, and I will give you life as your victor's crown (Revelation 2:10 NIV).

"If anyone is to go into captivity, into captivity they will go. If anyone is to be killed with the sword, with the sword they will be killed." This calls for patient endurance and faithfulness on the part of God's people (Revelation 13:10 NIV).

This calls for patient endurance on the part of the people of God who keep his commands and remain faithful to Jesus (Revelation 14:12 NIV).

Imagine a young man in college; he knows a big test is coming up, but one of his classmates convinces him that he will not have to take the test. In fact, every student who simply shows up for the test will get an A+. On the day of the test he goes to class fully expecting to be exempted, but is shocked when his teacher places the test on his desk, wishing him good luck. He ends up failing the test, because *he was convinced he did not have to prepare.*

The problem is that so many Americans do not have a place for persecution and suffering in their theology. I could list many Scriptures that state the opposite such as Matthew 13:21, Mark 10:30, Acts 8:1, and Second Timothy 3:12. In addition, when we look at the life of New Covenant believers (Paul, Stephen, James...), we see a tremendous amount of suffering for the sake of the kingdom. One primary reason that they were able to hold up under the suffering was that they knew it was for the glory of Yeshua. They understood that their *present sufferings* [were] *not worth comparing with the glory that will be revealed in* [them]" (Romans 8:18). They were not suffering for doing evil—they were targeted because of their testimony.

> *Many Americans do not have a place for persecution and suffering in their theology.*

Look at the attitude of the apostles after being beaten for "the Name":

> *They called the apostles in and had them flogged. Then they ordered them not to speak in the name of Jesus, and let them go. The apostles left the Sanhedrin, rejoicing because they had been counted worthy of suffering disgrace for the Name. Day after day, in the temple courts and from house to house, they never stopped teaching and proclaiming the good news that Jesus* [Yeshua] *is the Messiah* (Acts 5:40-42 NIV).

Several things jump out at us here:

1. It is God's will that we suffer for His kingdom.

2. It is God's will that we go through that suffering with joy.

3. Despite persecution, be it from the Sanhedrin or the Antichrist, we are to continue "teaching and proclaiming the good news" of Yeshua the Messiah.

I am not saying that we should look for suffering, or that if we are not suffering, we are not in God's will. What I am saying is that we must have a place for suffering in our theology. Not suffering tragic car accidents, sicknesses, or other calamities—but rather suffering for the kingdom. When Paul details the hardship he has endured in Second Corinthians 11, it is all in the context of missions work:

Five times I received from the Jews the forty lashes minus one. Three times I was beaten with rods, once I was stoned, three times I was shipwrecked, I spent a night and a day in the open sea, I have been constantly on the move. I have been in danger from rivers, in danger from bandits, in danger from my own countrymen, in danger from Gentiles; in danger in the city, in danger in the country, in danger at sea; and in danger from false brothers. I have labored and toiled and have often gone without sleep; I have known hunger and thirst and have often gone without food; I have been cold and naked (2 Corinthians 11:24-27 NIV).

Paul received the forty lashes not for *mischief*, but for *ministering*. He went days without food and nights without sleep not for *burglarizing*, but for *blessing*. This is what I mean by *kingdom suffering*. And Paul understood that when one

enters into Yeshua's suffering, one experiences intimacy with
Yeshua at a deeper dimension.

> *I want to know Christ* [Messiah]—*yes, to know
> the power of his resurrection and participation in his
> sufferings, becoming like him in his death* (Philippi-
> ans 3:10 NIV).

Paul understood that to *know Him* was to *suffer with Him*.

THE CHURCH'S RESPONSE

What is going to happen to all those people who have
been promised they will escape the coming persecution
when they have to choose between the mark of the beast and
Yeshua? Will they be ready? Will they be willing to suffer
for the kingdom? Will they be emotionally prepared to take
their stand?

Yeshua predicted that in the very last days many believers
would deny the faith in the face of persecution:

> *Then you will be handed over to be persecuted and put
> to death, and you will be hated by all nations because
> of me. At that time many will turn away from the
> faith and will betray and hate each other* (Matthew
> 24:9-10 NIV 2011).

Could it be that these who fall away are people who are
not ready for suffering—people who don't think it will happen to them? It is possible that these are those who expected
to escape, but didn't. Let's be honest—you are more likely
to withstand Tribulation if you have been preparing for it,
than if you have not. The ant survives the winter because he
prepares. The house built on the rock withstands the storm.

With this in mind, I appeal to those of you who believe in a pre-Tribulation Rapture to consider the argument put forth in the remaining pages of this chapter. My goal is not to convince you that *I am right,* but rather to save you from possible adversity. Listen—if I am wrong, great; I go to heaven seven years earlier than I anticipated! But if I am right—I want to be prepared for what could come.

Again—be ready to go, but also be prepared to stay.

> *You are more likely to withstand Tribulation if you have been preparing for it, than if you have not.*

Let me also make clear, in addition to the suffering—which will be primarily persecution from the Antichrist's forces, not the plagues or curses—the body of believers will be victorious. There is much in the Word to encourage us that whatever suffering we endure in the end times, it will be in the midst of worldwide revival. It will be the most exciting time in world history to be alive, to be a believer, and to preach the gospel! The message of Yeshua will reach the ends of the earth (see Matthew 24:14). Despite the attacks of the Antichrist and his forces, the gospel will overcome. Many will be saved. I don't believe that Yeshua returns for a defeated Bride, but an overcoming one! Why would anyone want to be raptured out of that?

HISTORY OF PRE-TRIBULATION POSITION

When dealing with controversial theology, I have a particular method to help me find the truth: Imagine you were completely ignorant about either view. Then you were handed a Bible and told, "Study this book and then give us your view of the end times." Understand that you have not been previously influenced, which allows you to view the Bible objectively. I have used this technique to help me understand God's Word on topics such as healing and miracles or speaking in tongues, but imagine that the subject was the timing of the Rapture. What are the chances that you would come away from your studying with the understanding that the Church would be raptured seven years prior to the Second Coming?

Ask yourself this question: If you had not been taught the pre-Tribulation theory, would you have come to that conclusion based on your own study of the Word? The answer is *probably not*. How would anyone, who was studying the Bible *uninfluenced*, come to the conclusion of two Second Comings? Or that the Church will suddenly disappear seven years prior to the return of the Lord? *There is not one explicit place where any Bible writer clearly spells this out.* I maintain that you would have to be taught this—that very few, if any, would come away with a pre-Trib theory.

You would have thought that the New Testament writers, and especially John the Revelator, would have made it clear. But it is not clear—not clear at all! Nowhere does John or any other writer explicitly say that the Church will be raptured seven years prior to the Second Coming. (This is why this doctrine was non-existent for eighteen hundred years.) So where did the pre-Trib view come from?

When studying the Scriptures, one of things we should always ask ourselves is, "How did the first believers understand this?" Concerning the Rapture, the consistent view of the believers for the first eighteen hundred years after the resurrection of Yeshua was that the Rapture and the Second

Coming were synonymous. There is no record of any theologian teaching this before the eighteen hundreds. Only then was this view popularized. And its origins are suspect.

> *Only then was the pre-Tribulation view popularized. And its origins are suspect.*

A widely held view espoused by authors such Dave MacPherson and Marvin Rosenthal (who had to resign his position as director of Friends of Israel because he left the pre-Trib camp) is that John Nelson Darby, considered by many the father of the pre-Trib theory, was influenced not by Bible study, but a prophecy of a young girl named Margaret MacDonald.

When young Margaret MacDonald was sick, she gave a series of supposed prophetic words. MacPherson claims that she prophesied about a secret Rapture of the church, while opponents say that if you read her words more closely, she actually was agreeing with a post-Tribulation Rapture. Of course the only things relevant are: 1) did John Darby visit MacDonald, and 2) was he influenced by her prophecy to create a new eschatology?

One of the very first things taught in a Bible Interpretation (exegesis) class is that you *never* establish a doctrine based on a prophecy! Joseph Smith is a prime example. Amazingly, some of the people who hold on to this doctrine so dearly are the very ones who do not believe that the gifts of the Spirit (prophecy) are for today. And when it comes to the Second Coming, we have an explicit WARNING not to be led astray by a *prophecy!*

> *Concerning the coming of our Lord Jesus Christ*
> [Yeshua the Messiah] *and our being gathered to*
> *him, we ask you, brothers and sisters, not to become*
> *easily unsettled or alarmed by the teaching allegedly*
> *from us—whether by a prophecy or by word or by*
> *letter—asserting that the day of the Lord has already*
> *come. Don't let anyone deceive you in any way...* (2
> Thessalonians 2:1-3 NIV).

Although Paul is referring to a specific false prophecy that had come forth in their day, the principle remains intact.

And to be clear, there are many scholars who reject the idea of Darby being influenced by a prophecy. They say it is merely coincidence that he popularized his pre-Trib theory after visiting Ms. MacDonald's church led by Edward Irving in the early 1830s.

Here is what we do know: John Darby, if not the first to preach a pre-Trib theory, was certainly the first to popularize it as part of his larger *dispensationalist* teachings. He is without a doubt the father of the pre-Tribulation Rapture theory, discovering something that Augustine, Luther, Calvin, Wesley, and others missed for eighteen hundred years after the resurrection.

The real issue here is the theology. Does it line up with the New Covenant? Will the Church be raptured from earth seven years before the Second Coming? Paul writes:

> *Concerning the coming of our Lord Jesus Christ* [Yeshua
> the Messiah] *and our being gathered to him...* (2
> Thessalonians 2:1 NIV).

So, we are clear that Paul begins the chapter speaking of *both* the Second Coming and the Rapture—of this, there can be no mistake. He goes on to refer to those two events as *one day* in verse 2.

> *...for that day will not come until the rebellion occurs and the man of lawlessness is revealed, the man doomed to destruction. He will oppose and will exalt himself over everything that is called God or is worshiped, so that he sets himself up in God's temple, proclaiming himself to be God* (2 Thessalonians 2:3-4 NIV).

Paul said *"that day," "...the coming of our Lord Jesus Christ* [Yeshua the Messiah] *and our being gathered to him,"* would not happen *until* the Antichrist is revealed and proclaims himself to be God in the Holy Temple. Scholars on both sides believe that the rebuilding of Temple (according to Daniel 9) will only begin and be completed in the midst of the Great Tribulation.

Let's be real clear: Paul calls the coming of Yeshua and the Rapture of His followers from earth, *"that day."* He doesn't say, "those days," but, *"that day."* I don't think we can create two separate events divided by seven years with the wording, *"that day."*

THE LAST TRUMPET

One of the most revealing passages concerning the Rapture can be found in First Corinthians 15:

> *Listen, I tell you a mystery: We will not all sleep, but we will all be changed—in a flash, in the twinkling of an eye, at the last trumpet. For the trumpet will sound, the dead will be raised imperishable, and we will be changed* (1 Corinthians 15:51-52 NIV).

This is a clear reference to the Rapture. It speaks of us, the believers, being changed—trading in our earthly bodies for a heavenly one. It even gives us the precise timing for the Rapture: *at the last trumpet.* Now all we have to do is find out when this *last trumpet* is sounded. I think one would be hard pressed to prove that the *last* trumpet actually occurs seven years before Yeshua's return. *How anti-climactic would that be?!*

There are several passages that refer to this trumpet. The Olivet discourse is considered the backbone of Bible prophecy. Most of the gospel writers allude to it. In Matthew 24, Yeshua mentions this end-times trumpet.

> *Immediately after the distress of those days "the sun will be darkened, and the moon will not give its light; the stars will fall from the sky, and the heavenly bodies will be shaken." Then will appear the sign of the Son of Man in heaven. And then all the peoples of the earth will mourn when they see the Son of Man coming on the clouds of heaven, with power and great glory. And he will send his angels with a loud trumpet call, and they will gather his elect from the four winds, from one end of the heavens to the other* (Matthew 24:29-31 NIV).

The first thing we notice is that He *"gather(s) his elect"* after *"the distress of those days."* The *"distress of those days"* is a clear reference to the Great Tribulation. The rapture occurs *after* this.

In addition, it is clear that the writer is referring to *one* event here. Most pre-Trib teachers believe that the rapture will be *secret*—people will just disappear. Everyone else will be left to try and figure out what happened. This is certainly the scenario put forth in most of the fiction novels written about the Tribulation period. Indeed the Bible speaks of it being a surprise, but it doesn't speak of it as being secret. In fact, Yeshua in Matthew 24 says that just *before* the rapture, there will be several visible signs in the sky:

1. Darkened sun and moon

2. Stars falling

3. Yeshua's sign in the sky

4. Yeshua visibly coming in clouds

Because of these signs, *"all the peoples of the earth will mourn"* (Matthew 24:30). This is not some secret event, but the greatest triumph known to humankind, heralded by the most amazing supernatural signs one could imagine. This is the Second Coming of Yeshua the Messiah! If it is a secret event, why are the nations mourning? They are mourning because they recognize that the One whom they have rejected is King over all the earth.

Revelation 1:7, which clearly refers to the Second Coming, coincides with Matthew 24:

> *"Look, he is coming with the clouds," and "every eye will see him, even those who pierced him"; and all the peoples of the earth "will mourn because of him." So shall it be! Amen* (Revelation 1:7 NIV).

1. The peoples of the earth mourn, according to Matthew, as the elect are gathered—or raptured.

2. And yet, every eye will see Yeshua. How could the Rapture be secret if "every eye will see him"?

Furthermore, if you read the Matthew passage, it does not appear or even hint that His *"coming on the clouds of heaven"* is separated by seven years from His angels who will *"gather his elect from the four winds."* It presents them as one event—or at least a series of events happening together. Now understand, Yeshua is the greatest theologian of all time—He created theology. He is Doctrine! He is the Word made flesh. How could it be that when Yeshua gives His most complete teaching of the Second Coming, He fails to mention that the Rapture will actually occur seven years earlier?

A THIEF IN THE NIGHT?

One might ask, "Doesn't the Bible say that He will come like a *thief in the night?* Doesn't that support the idea that the Rapture will be sudden and secret?"

That line of reason comes from First Thessalonians 5:

> *Now, brothers and sisters, about times and dates we do not need to write to you, for you know very well that the day of the Lord will come like a thief in the night. While people are saying, "Peace and safety," destruction will come on them suddenly, as labor pains on a pregnant woman, and they will not escape. But you, brothers and sisters, are not in darkness so that this day should surprise you like a thief. You are all children of the light and children of the day. We do not belong to the night or to the darkness* (1 Thessalonians 5:1-5 NIV).

This passage says nothing about a secret Rapture that will be a mystery to believers. Rather it simply says that *the world* will not expect it, as they are following the Antichrist. Yet when it comes, they will surely know it. It is hard to ignore sudden *"destruction"* that is as *"labor pains on a pregnant woman."* My wife has had three babies, and each time those labor pains came, it was obvious. Furthermore, Paul makes it clear that for the believers it will not be a surprise.

> *But you, brothers and sisters, are not in darkness so that this day should surprise you like a thief* (1 Thessalonians 5:4 NIV).

In summary, going back to Matthew 24 in the Olivet discourse, we see that the Second Coming and the Rapture are connected and *not separated by seven years.* We *know* that Yeshua is referring to the Rapture in Matthew 24 because He mentions: 1) the angels gathering His elect and 2) the trumpet. This would have to be the trumpet referred to in First Corinthians 15, because that is the *last* trumpet. This could not be a later trumpet because there is no later trumpet!

And yet, we can be confident that this passage refers to the Second Coming because Yeshua clearly states that *"they will see the Son of Man coming on the clouds of heaven, with power and great glory."*

REVELATION'S LAST TRUMPET

The last trumpet mentioned in Revelation is in chapter 11:

> *The seventh angel sounded his trumpet, and there were loud voices in heaven, which said: "The kingdom*

of the world has become the kingdom of our Lord and
of his Messiah, and he will reign for ever and ever"
(Revelation 11:15 NIV).

This passage refers to the initiation of God's wrath being poured out on the wicked, the coming kingdom of God, and the end of the age:

> *The nations were angry; and your wrath has come.*
> *The time has come for judging the dead, and for*
> *rewarding your servants the prophets and your people*
> *who revere your name, both great and small—and for*
> *destroying those who destroy the earth* (Revelation
> 11:18 NIV).

The references to *God's wrath, judging the dead* and *rewarding His servants*, coupled with the mention of *His kingdom coming* (see Revelation 11:15) put this trumpet right at the end of the Tribulation. We will see Yeshua coming in the clouds, the sun and moon will be darkened—then we, the body of Yeshua, will be raptured and meet Him in the clouds and be changed forever! This will happen even as He begins to pour out His wrath on the wicked and judge the nations (as we see in Revelation 19).

Then we will return with Him and reign with Him forever.

> **We will return with Him and**
> **reign with Him forever.**

The pre-Trib theory teaches that we meet Him in the sky, hang out in heaven for seven years, and then return to earth. The post-Trib theory teaches that we meet Him in the sky, are changed, and then return with Him and the saints who have gone before us, according to Revelation 19 and Zechariah 14, to judge the nations and then set up His messianic kingdom.

WHO ARE "THEY"?

In the most oft-quoted passage regarding the Rapture, it mentions a separate group of people apart from those who will be caught up.

> *According to the Lord's word, we tell you that we who are still alive, who are left until the coming of the Lord, will certainly not precede those who have fallen asleep. For the Lord himself will come down from heaven, with a loud command, with the voice of the archangel and with the trumpet call of God, and the dead in Christ will rise first. After that, we who are still alive and are left will be caught up together with them in the clouds to meet the Lord in the air. And so we will be with the Lord forever* (1 Thessalonians 4:15-17 NIV).

First off, let's note that again we see what appears to be the last trumpet—a trumpet blast that cannot be in two places at once. Here it is clearly signifying the Rapture, whereas in the other places it clearly signifies the Second Coming.

Second, he speaks about those who *"have fallen asleep,"* meaning believers who died waiting for Yeshua's return. When He returns, it says, after these saints are resurrected, we will meet *them* in the air—not just Him. While some hold to a soul-sleep belief (that believers who die are in an unconscious state), I believe that Paul uses the word "sleep" as a euphemism for not being physically alive. We know from Paul's teaching in Second Corinthians 5:6-8 and Philippians 1:23 that for the believer, death means entering the presence of God.[2]

Nevertheless, even if the saints are in heaven, something may be lacking regarding their final state that would cause them to still need to *"rise first."* And why would these sleeping saints experience resurrection seven years before the coming of the Lord? It makes much more sense that they experience this at His coming.

> *We receive our new glorified bodies and together,*
> *with Yeshua, return to set up the millennial kingdom!*

Either way, we meet *them* in the clouds with Yeshua. The next question is, if they are not returning with Him to earth (see Zechariah 14:3, Revelation 19:11), then why come with Yeshua? If we are being raptured to return to heaven for seven years, why are they making the trip? It is much more reasonable to see them as returning with Yeshua to greet us in the clouds, as we receive our new glorified bodies and together, with Yeshua, we return to set up the millennial kingdom! Oh what a glorious day that will be—for those raptured and those returned with Yeshua!

MORE ON THE LAST TRUMPET

The reference to the trumpet in Revelation 11:15 must be the trumpet referred to in First Corinthians 15:52, *the last trumpet*. And yet, this last trumpet, which *must* be sounded at the Rapture, is found here in Revelation at the *end* of the

Great Tribulation, not the beginning as the pre-Trib theory assumes.

Another problem with the idea of a pre-Trib Rapture is the trumpets found in Revelation 8:2. There are seven trumpet blasts that take place *after* the beginning of the Great Tribulation.

> *And I saw the seven angels who stand before God, and seven trumpets were given to them* (Revelation 8:2 NIV).

How can the *last* trumpet come *before* these seven? It can't. Therefore we must conclude that it is the last of these seven (see Revelation 11:15) that signifies the Rapture and initiates the Second Coming.

THE CHURCH WILL NOT SUFFER WRATH

Another main argument used to prove that the Rapture will take place before the Great Tribulation is derived from this passage:

> *For God did not appoint us to suffer wrath but to receive salvation through our Lord Jesus Christ* [the Messiah] (1 Thessalonians 5:9 NIV).

The premise is that God must remove us from earth before the Great Tribulation because He promised that we would not suffer His wrath.

It is true that God will not pour out His wrath—His anger—on Yeshua's Bride. He loves the Bride of Messiah. Wrath is reserved for His enemies. But the Great Tribulation is *not the wrath of God*. The wrath of God, as we just saw in Revelation 11:15, will be poured out on the wicked *at the end of the Great Tribulation.* Nowhere in Revelation does it ever mention the saints suffering the wrath of God, however it speaks numerous times about the saints suffering at the hands of God's enemies; and the hands of the Antichrist (see Revelation 6:9-11; 7:13-17; 12:11; 13:7-11; 17:6; 20:4).

The last trumpet will not only signify the Rapture, but the beginning of God's wrath on His enemies. But there is no indication that the Church will escape the Tribulation period and the persecution connected with it. We must separate the Great Tribulation from the wrath of God or the judgment—they are not the same. The Bible never promises believers a *Tribulation-free* life as some Western ministers suppose.

> *These things I have spoken to you, that in Me you may have peace. In the world you will have tribulation; but be of good cheer, I have overcome the world* (John 16:33).

Yeshua is telling His disciples how to maintain peace in the midst of tribulation, not how to escape it. In the parable of the sower, believers are not only promised tribulation, but persecution as well. Concerning the seed that fell on rocky soil He said:

> *Yet he has no root in himself, but endures only for a while. For when tribulation or persecution arises because of the word, immediately he stumbles* (Matthew 13:21).

Again, one must understand that persecution and trials *are not* tantamount to the wrath of God. It is true that Western believers are not used to persecution, but the fact remains that since the time of Yeshua, believers have been called thousands of times to lay down their lives for the Lord. Many have been tortured, ridiculed publicly, and stripped naked before their friends and family. Others were fed to lions. Even now, *before* the Great Tribulation, believers are suffering in China, Syria, Egypt, Nigeria, and so many other countries around the globe. Organizers of "Save the Christians," claim that 40 million believers have been killed for their faith in the twentieth century alone! "Each year 105,000 Christians die as martyrs—one new martyr every minute...."[3]

There is nothing unbiblical about believers suffering persecution for their faith. The fact that the Antichrist will pour out his anger at God upon the Church should not be surprising. The wrath of God poured out during the Great Tribulation is for the wicked. The body of believers will suffer the wrath of the Antichrist.

> *If anyone worships the beast and its image and receives its mark on their forehead or on their hand, they, too, will drink the wine of God's fury, which has been poured full strength into the cup of his wrath. They will be tormented with burning sulfur in the presence of the holy angels and of the Lamb. And the smoke of their torment will rise forever and ever. There will be no rest day or night for those who worship the beast and its image, or for anyone who receives the mark of its name* (Revelation 14:9-11 NIV).

It is the enemy, not God, who attacks the saints:

> *It* [the beast] *was given power to make war against God's holy people and to conquer them. And it was*

given authority over every tribe, people, language and nation. ...If anyone is to go into captivity, into captivity they will go. If anyone is to be killed with the sword, with the sword they will be killed. This calls for patient endurance and faithfulness on the part of God's people (Revelation 13:7,10 NIV).

Why do we need patient endurance? Because of Satan's wrath against the Church. We will not suffer *God's* wrath, but believers will be persecuted for their faith during the Great Tribulation. Consider Revelation 6:9-11 (NIV):

When he opened the fifth seal, I saw under the altar the souls of those who had been slain because of the word of God and the testimony they had maintained. They called out in a loud voice, "How long, Sovereign Lord, holy and true, until you judge the inhabitants of the earth and avenge our blood?" Then each of them was given a white robe, and they were told to wait a little longer, until the full number of their fellow servants, their brothers and sisters, were killed just as they had been.

This is why we are exhorted: *"the one who stands firm to the end will be saved"* (Matthew 24:13 NIV) and *"Be faithful, even to the point of death, and I will give you life as your victor's crown"* (Revelation 2:10 NIV).

No friend, we will not escape persecution as some teach, but to the ones who trust in the grace of God, the ones who stand firm, Yeshua Himself will reward you with the crown of life! Did not the prophet Daniel say many years before that the Antichrist would have authority to persecute the saints?

As I watched, this horn was waging war against the holy people and defeating them. ...He will speak against the Most High and oppress his holy people and try to change the set times and the laws. The holy people will be delivered into his hands for a time, times and half a time (Daniel 7:21,25 NIV).

WHAT ABOUT THE PLAGUES?

During the Great Tribulation there will be several awesome plagues that will come upon the earth. It is my opinion that the body of Messiah will not suffer from these plagues. There are incredible similarities between the plagues of Egypt and the plagues in Revelation. Dr. Daniel C. Juster, in his book *Revelation: The Passover Key*, articulately shows this connection. In the case of Egypt, the Israelites were protected. We have no reason to believe that under the New Covenant we will have less protection than those under the Old. In fact, when God protected the Israelites, they did not even have the Mosaic Law and its promises yet. How much more confidence should we have in light of promises like Second Peter 1:4 (NIV):

...he has given us his very great and precious promises, so that through them you may participate in the divine nature and escape the corruption in the world caused by evil desires.

One of the greatest tools that God will give us during the Great Tribulation for evangelism is the fact that, like the Israelites in Goshen, we will be unaffected by the plagues! It is believed that during the Exodus many Egyptians and slaves from other countries joined in with the Israelites (see Exodus 12:38). Certainly during the Great Tribulation, there will be places like Goshen where believers will be protected.

We, the body of Messiah, the believers,
will not suffer from these plagues.

Furthermore, when Paul speaks about the future Jewish revival in Romans 11 verses 12, 15, and 26, there is no mention of the Church being gone, but rather he speaks of a revival that I believe will outshine the book of Acts—one that will bring *"greater riches"* (than any other revival) and *"life from the dead."*

> *But if their* [Israel's] *transgression* [meaning, rejection of the gospel] *means riches for the world, and their loss means riches for the Gentiles, how much greater riches will their full inclusion bring! For if their* [Israel's] *rejection brought reconciliation to the world, what will their acceptance be but life from the dead?* (Romans 11:12,15 NIV)

Yes, in the midst of intense persecution and worldwide apostasy, there can and will be a great move of God. The greatest of all awakenings!

Contrary to those who teach that the last days will be merely a time of gloom and doom, I am convinced that the greatest harvest and revival the world has known will come during the Great Tribulation. Those disillusioned with the new Antichrist kingdom will turn to Yeshua, as they see a believing people unafraid, full of life, and willing to die for their faith.

WILL YOU BE READY?

Once again, I am not writing this to prove a point, but to suggest that we must be ready to live through the Great Tribulation. Even as there will be a great revival in the last days, there will be a great apostasy (see Matthew 24:10). I am convinced that it will partly come from those who were not ready for persecution who will so quickly deny their king. Their roots will not be deep; and when the heat of the Tribulation comes, they may fall away.

Is there any believer in the past hundred years more respected than Corrie ten Boom? She suffered horribly under the Nazis for rescuing Jews from Hitler. She had some very sobering words for those who think that the believers will be raptured out of this world before there is any tribulation:

> In China, the Christians were told, "Don't worry, before the tribulation comes you will be translated—raptured." Then came a terrible persecution. Millions of Christians were tortured to death. Later I heard a Bishop from China say, sadly, "We have failed. We should have made the people strong for persecution, rather than telling them Jesus would come first. Tell the people how to be strong in times of persecution, how to stand when the tribulation comes—to stand and not faint."
>
> I feel I have a divine mandate to go and tell the people of this world that it is possible to be strong in the Lord Jesus Christ. We are in training for the Tribulation, but more than 60 percent of the Body of Christ across the world has already entered into the tribulation. There is no way to escape it.

We are next.

In America, the churches sing, "Let the congregation escape tribulation," but in China and Africa the tribulation has already arrived. This last year alone more than two hundred thousand Christians were martyred in Africa. Now things like that never get into the newspapers because they cause bad political relations. But I know. I have been there. We need to think about that when we sit down in our nice houses with our nice clothes to eat our steak dinners. Many, many members of the Body of Christ are being tortured to death at this very moment, yet we continue right on as though we are all going to escape the tribulation.[4]

As a young believer I remember the first time someone explained to me about the idea of escaping earth before the Great Tribulation. I have to tell you I was dejected. It seemed to me that the Great Tribulation would be the ideal time to be an evangelist. I actually asked the Lord if I could stay. It wasn't that I wanted to suffer. I understood that God could take care of me. There is grace to suffer.

The key is to be ready to leave and to be ready to stay.

When Stephen was martyred, the Bible says he had the face of an angel. That is grace. God will not leave you alone. I am not seeking to scare you. If we prepare ourselves emotionally and spiritually, we will not be caught unaware.

Corrie ten Boom in the same letter shares:

When I was a little girl, I went to my father and said, "Daddy, I am afraid that I will never be strong enough to be a martyr for Jesus Christ."

"Tell me," said Father, "When you take a train trip to Amsterdam, when do I give you the money for the ticket? Three weeks before?"

"No, Daddy, you give me the money for the ticket just before we get on the train."

"That is right," my father said, "and so it is with God's strength. Our Father in Heaven knows when you will need the strength to be a martyr for Jesus Christ. He will supply all you need—just in time…"

The key is to be ready to leave and to be ready to stay.

ENDNOTES

1. It is my opinion that the Great Tribulation period will come directly after the Ezekiel 38-39 Gog and Magog War. God will draw Israel's enemies against them.

> *And I will turn thee back, and put hooks into thy jaws, and I will bring thee forth, and all thine army, horses and horsemen, all of them clothed with all sorts of armour, even a great company with bucklers and shields, all of them handling swords* (Ezekiel 38:4 KJV).

This invading army will be comprised of many Muslim nations and possibly Russia. It is interesting to note once God gives Israel victory over them, they will burn the invading armies' weapons for seven years—not six or eight, but seven, the number of years the Great

Tribulation will last.

Then those who live in the towns of Israel will go out and use the weapons for fuel and burn them up—the small and large shields, the bows and arrows, the war clubs and spears. For seven years they will use them for fuel (Ezekiel 39:9 NIV).

After this victory, Israel will make peace with her defeated foes. This peace will include the United Nations or whatever entity has control, to give Israel permission to rebuild her ancient Temple. We can assume that the Dome of the Rock and Al-Aqsa Mosque will be destroyed during the Ezekiel war, or maybe its destruction caused the war. But we know that in order for the Temple to be rebuilt, the mosque will be destroyed.

This deal will be brokered by a charismatic world leader—the Antichrist. Of course, he will be deeply loved and revered for bringing peace to the Middle East— finally. *"He* [the Antichrist] *will confirm a covenant with many for one 'seven'"* (Daniel 9:27 NIV). The peace will last three and one-half years—then he will reveal his true colors. *"...In the middle of the 'seven' he will put an end to sacrifice and offering. And at the temple he will set up an abomination that causes desolation, until the end that is decreed is poured out on him"* (Daniel 9:27 NIV). *"He will oppose and will exalt himself over everything that is called God or is worshiped, so that he sets himself up in God's temple, proclaiming himself to be God"* (2 Thessalonians 2:4 NIV). He will enter the Jewish Temple and declare Himself to be God or the Messiah. He will get away with such a claim because according to Revelation 13, he will die and rise from the dead.

> *One of the heads of the beast seemed to have had a fatal wound, but the fatal wound had been healed. The whole world was filled with wonder and followed the beast. People worshiped the dragon because he had given authority to the beast, and they also worshiped the beast and asked, "Who is like the beast? Who can wage war against it?"* (Revelation 13:3-4 NIV)

The Antichrist will persecute Israel and the saints as seen in Zechariah 14:1-2 and in this passage in Daniel:

> *As I watched, this horn was waging war against the holy people and defeating them. …He will speak against the Most High and oppress his holy people and try to change the set times and the laws. The holy people will be delivered into his hands for a time, times and half a time* (Daniel 7:21,25 NIV).

It is my belief that the two witnesses of Revelation 11 appear at this time to prophesy against the Antichrist and warn the world against following him. While many Bible teachers see their ministry taking place at the beginning of the Great Tribulation, I think they appear during the second half. Both views are valid, and one day we will know for sure.

The Antichrist finally overcomes them (after three and one-half years of them breathing fire against their enemies!). He rejoices at his victory and can now finally attack Israel. He gathers his armies in the valley of Mount Megiddo—or Armageddon (see Revelation

16:16). They march on Jerusalem and attack her (see again, Zechariah 14).

It would be silly to predict exactly how things play out, but the Jews of Jerusalem will cry out to Yeshua as he predicted in Matthew 23:37-39; He will then return to earth on a white horse with the saints in heaven (see Revelation 19:11). However, *"we who are still alive and are left will be caught up together with them in the clouds to meet the Lord in the air. And so we will be with the Lord forever"* (1 Thessalonians 4:17 NIV). We will be changed and given new bodies. We will return with Him as He comes to defend Israel and bring judgment on the nations. He will set up His millennial kingdom and the survivors from the nations (or at least delegations) will come to worship Him on the Feast of Sukkot (Tabernacles) (see Zechariah 14:16).

I realize that I just took a subject about which scholars write hundreds if not thousands of pages. Look up the passages and come to your own conclusion.

2.   "Who Are the Dead in Christ in 1 Thessalonians 4:16?" Got Questions Ministries, http://www.gotquestions.org/dead-in-Christ.html; accessed July 8, 2014.

3.   Edward Pentin, "Rally for the 40 Million Martyred Christians," Persecution.org, http://www.persecution.org/2012/07/30/rally-for-the-40-million-martyred-christians/; accessed July 8, 2014.

4.   Gavin Finley, "Corrie Ten Boom on the Rapture of the Church," Endtime Pilgrim, http://endtimepilgrim.org/corrie.htm; accessed July 8, 2014.

Chapter Eleven

"O, Jerusalem!"

David Brennan

My interest in current international political issues as they relate to biblical prophecy dates from my college days. I'm from New Orleans, and I earned a degree in political science from the University of New Orleans. I remember a friend who used to play tapes about biblical prophecy for me, but I was not a Christian yet, so I couldn't put it all together.

Then something life-changing happened. In the early 1990s, I was staying alone in an apartment in Florida while my family was back in New Orleans. Just a little earlier, an elderly woman had tried to talk to me about Jesus, but I didn't want to hear anything about Him. Still, in an effort to find some comfort for difficulties I was in, I found a Bible on a shelf in the apartment, and I took it down. I had never looked at one before, but since I had heard that the Bible could help in times of trouble, I tried to read it. I was disappointed to find that it didn't make any sense to me, so I just went to bed.

That night, I had a terrifying dream about a huge red dragon that was coming after me, and I woke up in a puddle of perspiration. (I didn't yet know anything about the dragon in the book of Revelation.) My heart was racing so fast I became concerned about my physical well-being. Eventually, after I had calmed down somewhat, I looked upward in the darkness of the bedroom and I decided to say the words of a prayer I had heard: "I accept Jesus Christ as my Savior." Then I went back to sleep.

I woke up the next morning, remembering what had happened. I saw the Bible lying there and I decided to give it another shot. This time it was easy to read, alive and intriguing. I couldn't put it down. Now what my friend had told me about Bible prophecy began to make sense. What a transformation!

From a political standpoint, I had always been a fan of Israel. From that point forward, I began to study biblical prophecies about Israel—and I could see that many of them were being fulfilled.

PLAGUES AND JUDGMENTS

I think it's fascinating the way real events corroborate biblical accounts. For example, take the Exodus of the people of Israel from Egypt. We are familiar with the whole Old Testament story of Moses and the ten plagues that the Lord visited on Egypt. Did you know that an ancient, non-biblical papyrus verifies the Bible account? It was written by a counselor in pharaoh's court, and it validates specific plagues, along with the fact that a large group of slaves became restive. The court counselor was named Ipuwer, and the document is called the Ipuwer Papyrus. It came to light in the early 1800s near the Egyptian pyramids, and today it is kept in the Dutch National Museum of Antiquities in Leiden, Netherlands.

> *The ten plagues represent clear examples of divine judgment falling hard on the nation of a political leader who dares to put himself against God's will for the people of Israel.*

Ipuwer writes in detail about horrible events such as water being turned to blood, events that we can recognize as the plagues recorded in the book of Exodus. The ten plagues represent one of the clearest examples of divine judgment falling hard on the nation of a political leader who dares to put himself against God's will for the people of Israel, specifically where the Promised Land is concerned. Pharaoh was trying to thwart the Israelites from possessing the land in the first place, and he probably lost his life as a result. His country was devastated.

Some additional hieroglyphics confirm what happened. In a museum north of Cairo you can view a huge, hieroglyphic-incised stone that is called the "El Arish stone" that is named after the place where it was discovered in 1887. The stone had probably been used as a shrine at one time, and it dates from the Ptolemaic period, although it describes events of twelve hundred years earlier—it tells the story of the Exodus from the point of view of the pharaoh. It describes the earlier pharaoh going to the Red Sea, to the same location where the Bible says the Jews camped when they first fled Egypt, and then how that pharaoh ended up being "lost" in a "whirlpool" of water.

CATASTROPHIC EVENTS

Now this ancient set of incidents is tremendously significant to this day, and here's why: Israel went on to establish a sovereign identity with national boundaries that at one time encompassed much more territory than we see today (and of course that shrank to nothing for a long time before being reestablished in 1948, when the modern state of Israel appeared). And every time efforts have been made to remove that land from Israel, historically significant disasters occur to the nation or group of nations that initiates the effort. These catastrophes occur suddenly.

I have been tracking them in particular since 1991, and in the process I have discovered that their timing closely mirrors the timing of international political actions that are negative against the Promised Land of Israel. It's very much like what happened to the pharaoh at the time of the Exodus; the disasters affect innocent citizens as well as the political leader(s) who have made some kind of declaration against Israel. Many of them are natural disasters such as storms, heat waves, or earthquakes. Other disasters come in the form of financial crashes and extreme disorders of communication in whatever part of the world the threat to Israel came from.

Such events would seem to be random, but a common denominator links them. It can be found in First Thessalonians 5:1-3 (KJV):

> *But of the times and the seasons, brethren, ye have no need that I write unto you. For yourselves know perfectly that the day of the Lord so cometh as a thief in the night. For when they shall say, Peace and safety;*

then sudden destruction cometh upon them, as travail
upon a woman with child; and they shall not escape.

That's what they all say: "Peace!" Political leaders want
to disentangle Palestine and Israel, in the process forcing
Israel to cede land in the name of peaceful coexistence. In
the name of peace, they are trying to orchestrate changes.
But what do they get instead of peace? They get destruction
every time, sudden destruction, often on the same day that
the declaration of peace was formulated or broadcast. You
can call these coincidences if you want to. But their number
is mounting up steadily. The warnings are going unheeded
by the people who need to hear them. It's like a broken
record: peace and sudden destruction, peace and sudden
destruction. As I see it, God is trying to warn people—"You
may *not* touch the apple of My eye, Israel!"

> *As I see it, God is trying to warn people—"You*
> *may not touch the apple of My eye, Israel!"*

That same passage goes on to urge believers to keep a sol-
emn watch:

> *You aren't in the dark about these things, dear brothers*
> *and sisters, and you won't be surprised when the day*
> *of the Lord comes like a thief. For you are all children*
> *of the light and of the day; we don't belong to darkness*
> *and night. So be on your guard, not asleep like the*
> *others. Stay alert and be clearheaded...* (1 Thessalo-
> nians 5:4-6 NLT).

That kind of a word implies that there's something to
watch for. We will be surprised by the *"day of the Lord"* only

if we have been lulled into complacency by all the talk of peace and safety.

FOUR HORNS

Staying alert and watchful involves coming to understand what certain biblical prophetic words mean regarding current events. For example, much speculation surrounds the meaning of the "four horns" and the "four carpenters" mentioned in Zechariah's prophecy:

> *Then lifted I up mine eyes, and saw, and behold four horns. And I said unto the angel that talked with me, What be these? And he answered me, These are the horns which have scattered Judah, Israel, and Jerusalem. And the Lord shewed me four carpenters. Then said I, What come these to do? And he spake, saying, These are the horns which have scattered Judah, so that no man did lift up his head: but these are come to fray them, to cast out the horns of the Gentiles, which lifted up their horn over the land of Judah to scatter it* (Zechariah 1:18-21 KJV).

Along with many others, I believe that this is being fulfilled today in the form of the Quartet (short for "Quartet in the Middle East"), which consists of a Palestine-Israel peace-brokering alliance between four political powers—the United States, Russia, the United Nations, and the European Union. The group was formed in Madrid in 2002 to mediate the peace process between Palestine and Israel; but in effect, they have come together to remove land from Israel, to weaken and scatter Israel.

Zechariah spoke in terms of four "horns" (which symbolize political power) going against the land in the plural, and then at the end it says, "lifted up their horn" (singular), which indicates that they act as one. This is the first time in the history of Israel that we have four powers acting as one to scatter the land of Israel. Some people think that Zechariah's prophecy refers to events that have now become history, but the facts show that any other alliances did not fulfill the word this well.

The prophetic word is a warning. It indicates that when this group of four horns does their thing to scatter the land of Israel, it is going to result in the "fraying," or destructive action against the nations that are represented by the horns. This is exactly what we have been seeing since the inception of the Quartet. Their first meeting was April 30, 2003, and that day was also the beginning of a month of the worst weather in U.S. history. You may remember it. As many as 562 tornadoes ripped through the midsection of the country, and more than 1,500 hailstorms pummeled U.S. citizens. This widespread disaster was not limited to the United States. After the worst weather ended in late May, Europe entered into their worst heat wave in 250 years. Something like 52,000 died as a result of it. You can call it a "coincidence" if you like, but I think it represents the "fraying" of two of those horns.

After talking about the four horns, Zechariah goes on to say, "*he that toucheth you* [Jerusalem] *toucheth the apple of his* [God's] *eye*" (Zech. 2:8 KJV). Any powerful entity that touches the land of Israel might as well have poked a finger into God's own eye. Retaliation ensues.

> *Any powerful entity that touches the land of Israel might as well have poked a finger into God's own eye.*

I would say that the "carpenters" are powerful angels who do God's bidding. We don't call storms "acts of God" for no reason. After all, He is the Creator of our natural world, and the Lord over it. He can do whatever He wants to, and He wants to make disasters memorable. He also controls human affairs on a global scale. That is why, in my view, we had the global financial meltdown. Look at the sequence of events.

The head of the Quartet, Tony Blair, first went to the Middle East on July 23, 2007, prior to what is called the Annapolis Peace Conference in November (which proved to be more or less a land bazaar; everybody wanted to get their hands on Israel's land). While no immediate action took place, they set up a framework that can be used in the future to remove the land. It was a significant gathering.

This was also the date on which the global financial meltdown began. In the same week of Tony Blair's visit to begin the effort to remove land from Israel, the premium paid by international banks to each other for borrowing money precipitated a financial liquidity crisis that could not be stopped until it became what is called a Sigma 6.2 event, something that should happen only once in every 2.5 million days. The financial crisis broke into public awareness the next year, in 2008.

BREAKING JUDGMENTS

Let me give you several other examples of catastrophes (out of at least thirteen, to date) which have been "coincidental" with declarations against the land of Israel. These events share the three key common-denominator words that I have already mentioned: "peace," "sudden," and "destruction."

At the end of October, 1991, just as U.S. President George H.W. Bush was opening the first Madrid "land for peace" Conference in Madrid, Spain, the original "perfect storm" (the one the movie came from) crashed into the New England coast. The monster storm spared nobody's property up and down the east coast of North America, including President Bush's Kennebunkport, Maine, home.

One year later, the Madrid peace talks resumed in Washington, DC, and anybody who was in Florida in August of 1992 will remember the ferocity of Hurricane Andrew, which at the time was the worst natural disaster ever to hit the United States.

Within two years, that record was challenged by the massive Northridge earthquake, 6.9 on the Richter scale, in Southern California. It struck a mere twenty-four hours after then-President Clinton had met with Syria's president, Hafez al-Assad, in Geneva, to discuss a peace agreement with Israel that would have involved Israel giving up the Golan Heights.

Throughout the year 1998 and into 1999, several major disasters, natural or otherwise, can be connected to the repeated, cool reception on the part of President Clinton and Secretary of State Madeleine Albright toward Israeli Prime Minister Benjamin Netanyahu, along with their warmer responses to Yasser Arafat.

*The U.S. landfall of the horrific Hurricane
Katrina in 2005 occurred just as the forcible
removal of the Jews from Gaza was completed.*

Moving into the next decades, we find ourselves on the
eve of the U.S. landfall of the horrific Hurricane Katrina
in 2005 just as the forcible removal of the Jews from Gaza
was completed. Then there was an unusual one: In 2010,
Great Britain ran an ad to build tourism for Israel. The ad
promoted travel to Eastern Jerusalem, and it showed a picture of the Western Wall. But they had to pull it on April
14 of that year. The Advertising Standards Authority of
the United Kingdom said that East Jerusalem is not part
of Israel but rather part of some future Palestinian state.
Naturally, this had an impact on tourism to Israel, but
then something unexpected had repercussions on tourism
throughout northern Europe—the eruption of the Eyjafjallajokull volcano in Iceland sent ash up into the atmosphere
and shut down airlines for days. It just goes to show what
can happen as a result of a major policy shift against Israel
and her territory.

On May 19, 2011, U.S. President Barack Obama made a
pro-Palestinian speech; he declared that Israel should revert
to its pre-1967 borders, which is something that previous
presidents would never have asked Israel to do. He also indi-
cated that he didn't want the newly created Palestine state
to be severed in two; he wanted it to be one continuous land
mass. Well, the problem with that is that Israel gets in the
way, so it means that Israel would have to bisected. This was
such a strong shift against Israel and previous U.S. policy
that even the normally supportive *Washington Post* detailed

its contradictions, and the Democrat leader of the Senate, Harry Reid, came out against it.

Alan M. Dershowitz, a noted Harvard law professor, called it a "mistake." The outcry was tremendous, and the backstory is fascinating. As anyone can figure out, the president did not come up with that policy overnight; it had been decided some time before. Only in retrospect can we figure out when. Unexpectedly, in a letter dated April 6, George Mitchell, the prominent Arab-American who had been the Special Envoy for Middle East Peace since 2009, had resigned. Most likely, the Obama administration's policy decision about Israel had occurred only a day or two before his resignation, which would put it on the fourth or fifth of April.

What else happened on April 4, 2011? The beginning of the worst tornado rampage in world history, to date. Hundreds of tornados were spawned by the weather system, something like 892, including the monster tornados that struck Joplin, Missouri, and four other cities. This historically significant, month-long calamity also included severe flooding, the likes of which had not occurred since 1927.

Don't you think it should be highly unusual to have your point man for the Middle East resign just prior to such a major announcement? The fact that Mitchell resigned just before the president's big speech indicates how strongly he felt against the policy. If we're reading the signals correctly, it appears that the God of Israel also feels strongly about it.

THE UNITED STATES LEADS THE CHARGE

Now we know that the God of Israel is a God of peace—but He's not a God of false peace. Even though the United

States of America is located geographically far away from the land of Israel and we may not ever be implicated directly in military combat, our leaders should be taking a warning from these events.

*The God of Israel is a God of peace—
but He's not a God of false peace.*

Point of fact: the United States has been leading the charge for dividing the land of Israel. All of these initiatives, taken under the guise of peace and fairness, have not produced any peace. What has been the fruit? Even when Israel's land has been removed and autonomy has been handed to Palestine, this action has done little to quell the clamor. In mosques, the preaching against Israel has never been harsher: "Destroy the Jews! They are not even human, but rather subhuman!" This is eerily similar to Nazi rhetoric in the 1930s.

Will we take the warning seriously? Or will "peace" followed by "sudden destruction" go around and around like a broken record until it's too late? The persistent reiteration of the warning has got to mean that something dire is coming. So many historically significant catastrophes in a row must be pointing to a cataclysm of the greatest magnitude. Someone who loves his country as much as I do hates to bring this kind of a message.

And where the land of Israel itself is concerned, I can imagine that all this "land for peace" talk could result in the actual *expansion* of the borders of Israel rather than the expected shrinkage to an indefensibly small footprint. After all, the much more sizable historic boundaries have yet to be regained. Israel may get much more land in the end, much the opposite of what the international community expects or wants. Their efforts will come to naught. Only sudden destruction is guaranteed for those who decide to take land away from Israel.

Jesus is returning very quickly. He's coming back soon. Therefore, when you read the Bible and these things *don't* sound strange to you, it will be because you have learned to expect them. Of course there are going to be disasters. But you are instructed to fear not.

Fear not! Your Lord is coming soon.

Chapter Twelve

THE REMNANT IN THE LAST DAYS

PAT SCHATZLINE

On Sunday morning, June 1, 2014, I awoke from a dream at 2:00 a.m. and jumped out of bed, expecting flood-waters to engulf me at any moment. In my dream, a great flood was covering the entire United States of America. My wife, Karen, and I were running up a mountain, and as we were climbing I was screaming to my wife that we must get everyone to higher ground lest the flood overtake them. I could see the water rising from the southeastern states and time was running out. It seemed as if no one would listen as I tried to sound the alarm. I awoke from the dream with tears flowing down my cheeks and my heart pounding inside my chest; I felt as if I had just run a marathon. Later I discovered that Karen had a similar dream.

After I gathered myself and realized that it was only a dream, I began to pray in the Spirit. Finally I implored God about my dream. I said, "Lord, You promised that you would never flood the earth again! Why did I dream that dream?" He said, "Son, I will never destroy the earth again with water. The dream that you had represents My Spirit being poured out one last time across America before I return for My Bride. Ready yourself! Declare that I am beginning a new thing! I will raise up My remnant!"

This was not the first time I had heard God speak to me about the "remnant." God had spoken this same message to me before, in May 2012. It was the Friday before Pentecost Sunday and I was in Dallas, Texas. That morning I had decided to go for a jog and pray before heading to speak at an event. While jogging, I suddenly heard God speak to me, "I will raise up My remnant to stand for truth through the power of the Holy Spirit!" The concept of "remnant" had never really crossed my mind before. As the Spirit of God overwhelmed me, I began to weep before the Lord. I said, "God, I have no idea what a remnant is, and I don't understand why You are telling me this."

HE WILL POUR OUT HIS SPIRIT

For years I have declared that we are on the cusp of a supernatural breakthrough in America and final great awakening of the Bride of Christ. I can remember having dreams and visions of this outpouring as far back as my teenage years. Could now be the time that was prophesied by Joel?

And afterward I will pour out My Spirit upon all flesh; and your sons and your daughters shall prophesy, your old men shall dream dreams, your young men shall see visions (Joel 2:28 AMP).

That day I began looking for the word "remnant" in God's Word. My spirit soared as I realized that throughout the Bible the remnant consists of the ones God uses to bring transformation in the darkest of times. From cover to cover the Bible is all about the remnant! The remnant simply refuses to bow to the plans of the enemy regardless of the persecution, opposition, and demonic manifestation that comes against them. The apostle Paul declared, *"So too at the present time there is a remnant, chosen by grace"* (Romans 11:5 ESV).

> *Throughout the Bible the remnant consists of the ones God uses to bring transformation in the darkest of times.*

What is a "remnant," anyway? Dictionaries define a remnant as something that is left over, what remains after something is used up, such as a fragment or scrap of cloth that remains unsold or unused at the end of a bolt. In both the Old Testament Hebrew and the New Testament Greek, the meaning of the word "remnant" has to do with people. A remnant is what remains from a group of people after most of the group has been destroyed or dispersed.

So you could say that the remnant, although it may appear to be small, is potentially very useful. As God's remnant, we are like a rag in God's hand, the remnant that He uses to clean up lives and transform this world. When God's remnant comes together, they are as beautiful to the Creator as a hand-made quilt, providing the warmth and comfort of the gospel to a needy world. The remnant is the group that has always stood firm in times when truth was absent. That excites me!

One day I was praying and God gave me what I call, "The Remnant Manifesto." The following are a few of the declarations:

- The remnant has found freedom in the arms of a loving Savior who has not only forgiven their past, but also now has authority over their future.

- The remnant knows that the I Am has now made them His.

- The remnant consists of the fatherless, the forgotten, and the freedom fighters whose pedigree is that of a scarred Savior.

- The remnant doesn't stop where they should have died because they know Jesus didn't.

- The remnant chooses to let go of past hurts in order to experience the freedom that comes with forgiving and moving forward.

- The remnant chooses to leave a life of compromise for the spirit of consecration.

- The remnant will not be swayed by the wind of compromise, will not stare into the eyes of revenge, and will not seek the approval of the populace.

- The remnant seeks holy justice with a passion for pursuing those who have fallen asleep with the knowledge of Him who awakens the dead.

- The remnant does not bow to culture but finds culture recreated by their passion for Jesus.

- The remnant walks among lost humanity, not screaming insults or provoking slander, but invading with light that which has known only darkness.

- The remnant includes the apostle with worn-out garments, the smiling prophet, the transparent pastor, the weeping missionary, the teacher with tools in hand, and the servant evangelist.

- The remnant understands the fruit of the Spirit is not a salad for a church potluck but rather the diet of a lifetime.

- The remnant knows the gifts of the Spirit are not for the evangelical, charismatic, and Pentecostal talent show but rather weapons of a dying leader who has chosen spirit over flesh and freedom over slavery.

- The remnant stands on truth until the shifting sand of compromise slides away to reveal the rock of salvation.

- The remnant does not walk in fear of people's retribution but rather in fear that humankind will never know the love of a Savior.

- The remnant always clashes with religion because they know that, throughout history, religion has always tried to be the noose around the neck of a Holy Spirit movement.

- The remnant does not consist of pulpiteers or public speakers, but rather resuscitators of life to those who have lost breath.

- The remnant doesn't need the stage, but rather a place to call home to which to bring a weary guest.

- The remnant is satisfied at all times, hungering and thirsting after righteousness—and being filled.

- The remnant does not walk in flattering circles but rather in the places where the unknown sojourner must be found.

- The remnant says yes to the cross and no to the applause, yes to the altar and no to arrogance, yes to the covenant and no to worldly concepts.

The Remnant Manifesto is not for those who are not willing to pay a price. The late Pastor David Wilkerson wrote of the importance of the remnant rising up. He declared:

All the prophets saw the end times and prophesied of the gathering of a separated, holy people who would have great understanding in the Word of the Lord. Daniel heard great things from God but "understood not" (Daniel 12:8). However, he saw a day coming when a purified, tried and tested remnant would understand; there would be a last-day company full of wisdom and discernment in the things of God. "Many shall be purified, and made white, and tried; but the wicked shall do wickedly: and none of the wicked shall understand; but the wise shall understand" (Daniel 12:10).[1]

In the midst of the cultural darkness in which we now live, I believe that the remnant is the last hope for this world.

One day while praying, God put in my heart that things will get particularly rough for the Christians in the United States and around the world beginning in October 2016. I do not know what will happen during this time, but I do believe that our days of freedom of religion are numbered. I also believe that the day will come when martial law will be declared and the government will restrict gatherings of Christians. Already, we must be very guarded about speaking out against perversion, homosexuality, and the death of children in the womb by abortion.

> *Now is the time for the remnant to stand firm and declare the Word of God without hesitation, because the world is spinning toward a dangerous end-times war.*

Now is the time for the remnant to stand firm and declare the Word of God without hesitation, because the world is spinning toward a dangerous end-times war. Israel is now isolated; Russia is on the march invading neighboring nations; Islamic fundamentalism has reached a point of critical mass; and America is fiscally and morally bankrupt.

THE CHURCH AS REMNANT

What of the beautiful Bride of Christ? Where is the Church concerning these matters? Surely the Bride is making a stand, right? Does she not have a part to play in turning the tide? I believe that she does, but she must wake up before it is too late. The Bridegroom is at the door and He is looking for the virgins who have trimmed their lamps, filled them with oil, and waited attentively for His knock (see Matthew 25). We are now living in a time when a social gospel and false grace have driven truth from the houses of worship. Secular Christianity has taken root, proclaiming (at best) a non-confrontational message of humanism. A majority of churches now teach tolerance and relevance as their core values rather than holiness and repentance.

The remnant is called to rise up and lead a Holy Spirit revolution. It is time to wake up! It is time for the church to follow the charge of Second Chronicles 7:14 (ESV): *"If my people who are called by my name humble themselves, and pray and seek my face and turn from their wicked ways, then I will hear from heaven and will forgive their sin and heal their land."*

God has a word for us to declare. No more slumber! No more living your life in a daze! Pay attention to the admonishment of Romans 13:11-14 (MSG):

> *But make sure that you don't get so absorbed and exhausted in taking care of all your day-by-day obligations that you lose track of the time and doze off, oblivious to God. The night is about over, dawn is about to break. Be up and awake to what God is doing! God is putting the finishing touches on the salvation work he began when we first believed. We can't afford to waste a minute, must not squander these precious daylight hours in frivolity and indulgence, in sleeping around and dissipation, in bickering and grabbing everything in sight. Get out of bed and get dressed! Don't loiter and linger, waiting until the very last minute. Dress yourselves in Christ, and be up and about!*

Praying one morning, I heard the Holy Spirit say, "Pat, there's been a demonic onslaught sent from hell to make

Christian leaders believe they must live like the world to win the world."

This makes our message no longer clear that sin is sin and that God is *"a rewarder of those who diligently seek Him"* (Hebrews 11:6). "We preach tolerance instead of the wages of sin because socially it is received better."[2] To believe that you can partake in the lifestyle of those you are called to win means you are being seduced once again by what Jesus set you free from. God is calling His people back to supernatural encounters, not just theatrical gatherings and talks about self-reliance. We must awaken to our own depravity and know that time is running out. Nice messages and catchy sermonettes have never set a person free from the depths of sin.

> *God is calling His people back to supernatural encounters, not just theatrical gatherings and talks about self-reliance.*

Only a God-encounter on a national level will change our course. We must recognize that without Jesus setting us free from a life of sin we would be left to the same demise as the demons. This is nothing new. Jeremiah wrote how the people of Israel had lost their way and his words could apply to America. The man who wrote the book of Lamentations put it this way:

> *Your prophets courted you with sweet talk. They didn't face you with your sin so that you could repent. Their sermons were all wishful thinking, deceptive illusions* (Lamentations 2:14 MSG).

I believe that it is the goodness of God that draws people back to Him (see Romans 2:4), but it is also confession that brings us before God's throne (see James 5:14). And yet truth is now considered hate speech and our culture is declaring that God's Word can be amended by perversion. The outpouring of the Holy Spirit is considered a sawdust trail crusade that couldn't possibly be relevant. Altars have been relegated to the back rooms of modern churches, while pre-engineered services have all but fired the Holy Spirit from doing His job.

We must awaken before the prophecy of Matthew 24 comes to pass. Jesus told His disciples:

> *But as the days of Noah were, so also will the coming of the Son of Man be. For as in the days before the flood, they were eating and drinking, marrying and giving in marriage, until the day that Noah entered the ark, and did not know until the flood came and took them all away, so also will the coming of the Son of Man be. Then two men will be in the field: one will be taken and the other left. Two women will be grinding at the mill: one will be taken and the other left. Watch therefore, for you do not know what hour your Lord is coming. But know this, that if the master of the house had known what hour the thief would come, he would have watched and not allowed his house to be broken into. Therefore you also be ready, for the Son of Man is coming at an hour you do not expect* (Matthew 24:37-44).

ARE YOU READY?

We know that God has always saved for Himself a remnant, the ones who understand the times they live in and realize that God has marked them to lead. These are the ones who will not bow to the spirit of the world no matter what the enemy does to destroy them. The 144,000 Jewish believers whom God will rescue and use to evangelize and welcome Him back to the earth at the end of the Tribulation are part of the remnant (see Revelation 7:4 and Revelation 14). The remnant speaks with His voice.

Are you willing to be part of His remnant? If you can answer yes, then the following are your guidelines to being the remnant of the last days!

1. God's remnant chooses a life of consecration. God has always looked for those who are willing to belong to Him completely. This requires a lifestyle that is consecrated and holy. You cannot belong to the world and also be part of God's remnant. To be consecrated means to be separate. Jesus described what it means:

> *Now I'm returning to you. I'm saying these things in the world's hearing so my people can experience my joy completed in them. I gave them your word; the godless world hated them because of it, because they didn't join the world's ways, just as I didn't join the world's ways. I'm not asking that you take them out of the world but that you guard them from the Evil One. They are no more defined by the world than I am defined by the world. Make them holy—consecrated—with the truth; your word is consecrating truth. In the same way that you gave me a mission in the world, I give them a mission in the world. I'm consecrating myself for their sakes so they'll be truth-consecrated in their mission* (John 17:13-19 MSG).

You and I have been set apart for a purpose. We must be separate from the world. We must make up our minds to look like Jesus and nothing else. No more compromise. God wants all of you—not just part of you. Here's how the apostle Paul put it:

> *I don't want you to become part of something that reduces you to less than yourself. And you can't have it both ways, banqueting with the Master one day and slumming with demons the next. Besides, the Master won't put up with it. He wants us—all or nothing. Do you think you can get off with anything less?* (1 Corinthians 10:20-22 MSG)

2. God's remnant is usually the most "unqualified." *"Hosea put it well: I'll call nobodies and make them somebodies; I'll call the unloved and make them beloved. In the place where they yelled out, 'You're nobody!' they're calling you 'God's living children'"* (Romans 9:25-26 MSG). God doesn't choose the best in the crowd, most organized, most eloquent speakers, or the most likely to succeed. No! He chooses people like you and me who are simply available. Here is one of my favorite verses in the Bible:

> *Take a good look, friends, at who you were when you got called into this life. I don't see many of "the brightest and the best" among you, not many influential, not many from high-society families. Isn't it obvious that God deliberately chose men and women that the culture overlooks and exploits and abuses, chose these "nobodies" to expose the hollow pretensions of the "somebodies"?* (1 Corinthians 1:26-28 MSG)

The truth is that all of us are unqualified, but with God's help we will finish this life with nothing left to do. Let's stop declaring we're not qualified and start saying, *"with God all things are possible!"* (Matthew 19:26).

3. God's remnant looks forward, not backward. The apostle Paul declared that we must forget what is behind us (see Philippians 3:13). God has called us to dive into our future with hope, joy, and passion to transform this world. There is no going back, anyway! And God has promised us that He will reward our service: *"For God is not unjust so as to overlook your work and the love that you have shown for his name in serving the saints, as you still do"* (Hebrews 6:10 ESV).

We must stand firm regardless of what we face. James wrote, *"Blessed is the man who remains steadfast under trial, for when he has stood the test he will receive the crown of life, which God has promised to those who love him"* (James 1:12 ESV). God has a greater reward for you than the world could ever offer. His reward comes on the day of accountability when we will receive crowns that we will be allowed to throw at His feet. Those crowns will be adorned with the jewels of souls that we helped lead to the cross.

4. God's remnant pursues Holy Spirit encounters. I have always said that when we get to heaven our lifestyle should not change. God has called us to behold Him and in doing so we will become like Him. We must live our lives continually seeking God. This is the only way we will make it in the last days. Paul wrote:

> ...*God is a living, personal presence, not a piece of chiseled stone. And when God is personally present, a living Spirit, that old, constricting legislation*

is recognized as obsolete. We're free of it! All of us! Nothing between us and God, our faces shining with the brightness of his face. And so we are transfigured much like the Messiah, our lives gradually becoming brighter and more beautiful as God enters our lives and we become like him (2 Corinthians 3:17-18 MSG).

God has the ability to transform our darkest situation with one encounter. It is in the encounter that everything changes.

5. God's remnant always declares the truth. We must not hide from the tough issues. God has called us to declare truth and freedom. It is the truth that will set humankind free (see John 8:32). As we stand firm in the truth, we are not swayed by culture or opinions. The apostle Paul understood this when he wrote:

This is a terrific responsibility. Is anyone competent to take it on? No—but at least we don't take God's Word, water it down, and then take it to the streets to sell it cheap. We stand in Christ's presence when we speak; God looks us in the face. We get what we say straight from God and say it as honestly as we can (2 Corinthians 2:16-17 MSG).

God has entrusted us with His message and we must prove faithful. Humanity hangs in the balance and heaven is watching.

6. The remnant knows that God is with them at all times. Such freedom comes with knowing that you never walk into a room alone. God is with us in all circumstances.

As things get progressively rough in the last days, you must be sure of one thing—God is for you! He stands right beside you. Here is the greatest passage in the Bible for protecting your God-given authority:

> *Finally, be strong in the Lord and in the strength of his might. Put on the whole armor of God, that you may be able to stand against the schemes of the devil. For we do not wrestle against flesh and blood, but against the rulers, against the authorities, against the cosmic powers over this present darkness, against the spiritual forces of evil in the heavenly places. Therefore take up the whole armor of God, that you may be able to withstand in the evil day, and having done all, to stand firm. Stand therefore, having fastened on the belt of truth, and having put on the breastplate of righteousness, and, as shoes for your feet, having put on the readiness given by the gospel of peace. In all circumstances take up the shield of faith, with which you can extinguish all the flaming darts of the evil one; and take the helmet of salvation, and the sword of the Spirit, which is the word of God, praying at all times in the Spirit, with all prayer and supplication. To that end keep alert with all perseverance, making supplication for all the saints* (Ephesians 6:10-18 ESV).

When we are dressed in the authority that Jesus walked in, walking with Him, we help establish His kingdom.

7. God's remnant walks in the supernatural. Walking in the supernatural, we always expect God to do things beyond our control. It is time for signs and wonders. Supernatural power can change the most hardened heart. It is time to rely, not on ourselves, but on the person of the Holy Spirit!

God still keeps His promises!

> *For the seed shall be prosperous, the vine shall give its fruit, the ground shall give her increase, and the heavens shall give their dew—I will cause the remnant of this people to possess all these* (Zechariah 8:12).

> *Then the remnant left in Israel will take their place among the nations. They will be like dew sent by the Lord or like rain falling on the grass, which no one can hold back and no one can restrain. The remnant left in Israel will take their place among the nations* (Micah 5:7-8 NLT).

ENDNOTES

1. David Wilkerson, "A Revival of Cleansing," September 17, 2013; http://sermons.worldchallenge.org/en/node/24319; accessed July 10, 2014.

2. See my article, "The Problem With Being Relevant," Charisma Magazine, March 2014; http://www.charismamag.com/spirit/church-ministry/19759-the-problem-with-being-relevant; accessed July 10, 2014.

Chapter Thirteen

How to Prosper in the End Times

by Dr. Jim Richards

As we approach the Last Days, one of the most important questions we need to ask ourselves is concerning the goodness of God. We have to know we are clear on the fact that God is good, that He is *always* good, and that He can *always* be trusted in whatever situation we encounter. He always wants the best for us. And because God is always good, if we'll follow Him with our whole heart, then He will always lead us away from lack and into a place of abundance.

The psalmist declared, *"The LORD is my shepherd; I shall not want"* (Psalm 23:1). That last phrase could also just as easily be translated, "I shall not lack." If God doesn't lead us into lack, then what does He lead us into? He leads us into green pastures, beside still waters, to a table that has been prepared for us, and safely through the valley of the shadow of death. "I shall not lack" is a declaration that is as clear as the nose on our face about God always being good toward us.

Many Christians have misread portions of the Old Testament and have developed a negative concept of God. They are really not sure if they can trust Him. But I want to assure you: We can trust Him, and His promises work in any and every situation. He is completely good to us.

Even in the midst of trying circumstances, God has always shown His goodness by providing for His people. The children of Israel, who had been in slavery for hundreds of years, came out of the land of Egypt carrying great wealth. Joseph, a man who was kidnapped, tossed into a pit, sold into slavery, and ended up in prison, was delivered and raised up to a place of prominence by God in order to save the nation of Israel. And Daniel and the Hebrew children who were taken captive, and who were persecuted for their beliefs, were delivered by God and powerfully used in the nation of Babylon.

When there was a great famine in the land, *"Isaac sowed in that land, and reaped in the same year a hundredfold; and the LORD blessed him"* (Genesis 26:12). Isaac's prosperity began to grow until he became so wealthy that he had flocks that were the envy of the Philistines and the people around him, and he began to step into the wealth that God had promised to him through His covenant with Abraham. Whether we go through times of feasting or times of famine, we can always trust God—we can always follow Him.

While we know God is good, we have been influenced by the propaganda that is being fed to us by the governments of the world and by the news media, trying to cause us to fear and to feel like we can't trust God. All the plagues, famines, and shortages of our generation—and even those that will be created by the antichrist—are all manmade plagues. They are all shortages that are generated by the powerbrokers who are seeking to take control of the world, not by God.

Governments know they have to create crises in order for people to be willing to give up their rights and freedoms. One of the lies that they spread is the lie of lack—that there is not enough food and there are not enough resources for everyone to be sustained. Anything that can cause the population to feel insecure and unsafe is being propagated through the media.

This is essentially where the world is going in the Last Days, and there is no getting around it. Some people become afraid when they hear these things, but let me encourage you: You can trust God and walk with Him, and you can enjoy a full and abundant life in the midst of it all.

The Bible tells us that the antichrist will bring tribulation to the world for three and-a-half years, and then the last three-and-a-half years of the "seven-year tribulation" is God bringing tribulation on the antichrist and his nations. The Lord Jesus will ultimately return and establish His Kingdom upon the earth. And for a thousand years we will have the opportunity to see what it looks like for true righteousness to rule on this planet.

In the midst of these end times, the principles of prosperity and success are not only still intact, they must be adhered to more than ever before. Ecclesiastes 11:4 says, *"He who observes the wind will not sow, and he who regards the clouds will not reap."* In other words, if we put all of our attention on the circumstances surrounding us, we're not going to sow and we're not going to reap because we're living in fear.

When you "walk through the valley of the shadow of death," you have to think about whether or not you trust the person who is leading you. If you trust God, then you will depend on Him through all of the highs and lows, you will rely on Him, and you will partake of His resources in the midst of troubling times. That is what we are seeking to do as we follow God into true prosperity and success.

Success is about the capacity to see and seize opportunities. Again, Ecclesiastes says, *"The race is not to the swift, nor the battle to the strong, nor bread to the wise, nor riches to men of understanding, nor favor to men of skill; but time and chance happen to them all"* (9:11). I will never forget reading this verse and writing in the margin of my Bible, "But the question is, 'Do I recognize—do I see and seize—opportunity when it comes to me?'"

The answer to this question is all about whether or not we have a heart for success, a heart to prosper—and I'm not talking about having money just falling out of our pockets. I don't know what you think about when you think of prosperity, but I think of having enough for me, for my family, and enough to be a blessing and help to other people. More than just my temporal needs being met, I know and believe that God is my source, that He takes care of me, and that He is my provider. If you have a heart for success and recognize God as your provider, then you will see and seize opportunity as it comes to you.

Back in 2006 I began to see the change that was coming to the American economy and I took steps to prepare for it. I sold almost all of our ministry property, and I got our ministry as near debt-free as I possibly could. Also, the Lord impressed on me that I was to prepare believers to prosper during hard times.

Even though God created us for success, we are being systematically programmed to believe in failure. Just about anybody can prosper during good times. During most of the past forty years, anyone who showed up at work, and was faithful and dependable, could make a good living and have more than enough. But in hard times, the general laws of success are altered by the conditions in the world. In the current financial times, we need to be able to hear and follow the voice of God to know how to succeed in our unique situation.

> *Even though God created us for success, we are being systematically programmed to believe in failure.*

The Bible talks a lot about the need for wisdom. And wisdom, whether it's in the New Testament or the Old Testament, is always connected to practical application. Many people have the Word of God in their head, but they don't know how to apply it in a given situation to get the best outcome. The Bible tells us that real wisdom comes from the mouth of God. Only God has the capacity to know all the variables in our changing economy—the people we can trust, the people we can't trust, and what we actually have the faith, the physical strength, and the opportunity to do. God knows and sees all of these variables, and He can bring them together in one decision. The key is that we have to be alive to God in our heart, and we have to be able to recognize the voice of God when He is speaking to us.

People ask me, "What should I be investing in right now?" The answer is different for every person, partly based on what area of the country you're in and partly based on the circumstances surrounding you. This is about you following God from your heart in your particular situation—about making decisions that God has called you to make. Yes, you're going to need a general, cognitive knowledge of different aspects and markets; but true prosperity is only going to come from following God with your heart.

I have prospered in many of my endeavors over the past forty years. I have built numerous small businesses, all of which have been successful, and I have built them because I listened to the voice of God in my heart. Then I applied the principles for success and prosperity, particularly those found in the book of Proverbs.

> *True prosperity is only going to come*
> *from following God with your heart.*

One of the reasons for this success is that all of the financial boundaries I have in my life are based on my beliefs. This has nothing to do with the circumstances that surround me, it has nothing to do with my education (or the lack thereof), and it has nothing to do with who I know (or don't know). Even though all of those things come into play, the book of Proverbs says, *"Keep your heart with all diligence, for out of it spring the issues of life"* (Proverbs 4:23). "Issues" could just as well have been translated "boundaries." Out of our heart spring the boundaries for our life.

All of the boundaries we face in life are boundaries that we impose upon ourselves because of our beliefs. We often think that we are merely the sum total of our life experiences including everything we've succeeded in and everything wherein we've failed. Each time we are faced with an opportunity, in a nanosecond, our mind evaluates the situation in light of all of these past successes and failures, and it tries to convince us whether or not we can succeed.

We must remember that if we are in Jesus, we are a new creation. In Jesus we can yield to the wisdom and the power of God working in our hearts. Our natural tendency is to give people in authority influence over our lives, somehow letting them mold and shape us into the people we become. But no one else can write on our heart; nobody can create beliefs in our heart that inform our boundaries. God created us to where only we can create the beliefs of our heart by what we think about, what we ponder, and by the judgments that we pass against ourselves.

In walking out who we are as a new creation in Messiah Jesus, we have to deal with what our parents said to us, what they said about us, and their successes and failures. Their experiences have become our understanding of normal. Then we are influenced by what educators have taught us. If you're under forty years old, you have been systematically deceived by the public educational system. You were taught that socialism was good, even though the whole concept of socialism goes against God's Word that tells us to go out and multiply, prosper, and succeed.

God created this world to sustain humankind. As long as humanity is here and operating in the Word of God, we will be sustained and be able to live life to the fullest. Our whole concept of what happens when Jesus comes back is largely false. We have an idea that Jesus comes back and everybody immediately goes to heaven or hell upon His return. But this is not what actually happens. Jesus comes back and establishes His Kingdom upon the earth, and for a thousand years He rules and reigns in righteousness. The ungodly on the earth will get the chance to see what the world would look like ruled in righteousness, and they will discover that there are more than enough resources for the world to continue. And, amazingly, at the end of the thousand years the wicked will rise up and say, "We don't want righteousness." Then there's one last great rebellion where Satan is totally and completely overthrown. That's where the end of the world comes, not when Jesus first returns.

There are religious leaders who have convinced us it's ungodly to prosper; that there's something wicked about even wanting to do well in life. All of these teachings have influenced us, and then through our self-talk we have programmed ourselves to believe these lies that are totally inconsistent with the hundreds of Scriptures that tell us about God's desire for us to prosper.

How do you overcome these limiting beliefs in your life? First and foremost, you've got to let Jesus be your Lord, be your Shepherd. If you trust Him as your Lord, then you will follow Him and do what He tells you to do. If you don't trust Him, then you won't follow Him—you won't even be listening for His voice. So I want to encourage you to read the Scriptures, renew your mind, and meditate and ponder on the promises of God. God's Word is the key for us to be sustained in the Last Days.

Peter reminds us: *"His divine power has given to us all things that pertain to life and godliness, through the knowledge of Him who called us by glory and virtue, by which have been given to us exceedingly great and precious promises, that through these you may be partakers of the divine nature, having escaped the corruption that is in the world through lust"* (2 Peter 1:3–4). Every promise God has ever given needs to be highlighted in our Bible, and we need to read them over and over again. Every time we read one, we need to say, "This promise is mine because I am in Jesus."

It is important to not try to control the process. Success in today's economic environment isn't like anything we've ever seen before, and it's constantly changing. All that we know about success is based on the successes that we've had in the past. And while that is convenient, and there are some practical things we can learn from that, our tendency is that we rely only on our mental capacities.

But our mind has only one goal, and that is to protect our ego, to preserve our idea of who we think we are. If we follow only our intellectual mind, then we're going to be locked into whatever our life pattern is. This is where we have to say "no" to self and "yes" to God, and then acknowledge that we are a new creation in Messiah Jesus. We also need to develop some of the traits for success, the two most powerful traits being adaptability and flexibility, which come about because of self-confidence and self-worth.

We also have to develop a faith for success. We need to choose the outcome we desire. If we don't choose it, then God can't bless it. God is always limited to our free will. Even the Bible talks about how the children of Israel *"limited the Holy One of Israel"* (Psalm 78:41).

If we're going to have the faith of God, we've got to see the end from the beginning. We need to experience seeing ourselves living that end, seeing ourselves being prosperous, protected, and delivered. This has to become more real to us than anything else because this is what brings us to the place of belief and trust.

Faith in the heart is always immovable. In fact, that's one of the ways you know you've reached a place of true faith in your heart—you're immovable. You're not being stubborn, you're not being obstinate—you just believe the truth. This is why the Bible continually cautions us that we are not to doubt, because doubting is wavering. Wavering occurs when you start looking at the circumstances or the situations that oppose the Word of God. And when you find yourself wavering, that is when you need to go back and look at the end, and see the end from the beginning.

Once you are reminded of the end, you use your authority to bind and loose. Confession is a form of binding and loosing, because the word *confess* means to "say the same thing." Speaking to the mountain and telling it to move is where you are using your authority that Christ has entrusted to you. It is up to us to declare lawful those things that God has declared lawful, and to declare unlawful those things God has declared unlawful in our life.

We must be fully persuaded in our heart that the promises of God are not only true, but they're true for us. Take Scriptures about your identity in Christ, and use them to worship, to pray, and to meditate on so that you write the truth of God's Word on your heart in a way that you become immovable. And then, always follow the Holy Spirit in your heart. Don't follow the circumstances, don't look for external signs; learn to hear, know, and trust the voice of God.

Finally, don't wait to start applying these principles. Jeremiah 12:5 says, *"If you have run with the footmen, and they have wearied you, then how can you contend with horses?"* In other words, you'd better learn to stand on the promises of God now before things get worse. Develop generosity in your life now. Get the grace of God for prosperity working in your heart now. Listen to and obey the Holy Spirit as He leads you now. See yourself having all of your needs met and the desires of your heart fulfilled now: God protecting you, God leading you. When you lay your head on your pillow at night, imagine yourself being led by God, hearing the voice of the Holy Spirit, and following and trusting God.

There will be no generalized formula for how to succeed when we face these times that lay ahead of us. There will only be our willingness to hear and trust and follow the voice of God as He speaks to our heart.

Let me lead you in this prayer:

> *Father, in the name of Jesus, cause faith to come alive in me that I will stand up and break the strongholds of poverty in my life by declaring Your Word to be true for me. I pray for the wisdom and the leadership to find freedom from lack and to overcome debt. I thank You, Lord God, that the Holy Spirit is giving me great ideas for prosperity and success. I thank You that my heart is coming alive to what a good, dependable and faithful Father You are. I declare that I will trust You and follow You with all of my heart. In the Name of Jesus, Amen.*

ARE YOU READY FOR YOUR FINAL DAY ON EARTH?

SID ROTH

I have investigated the supernatural for more than forty years. What you are about to read is the most incredible supernatural event I have ever researched.

Isaiah, the great Jewish prophet, lived more than 2,700 years ago. Isaiah was supernaturally transported into the last day on earth. John, the great New Testament prophet, was also transported to see the final day on earth. What if I told you there is someone alive today who saw these same events—and that he saw them before he knew of Isaiah's and John's visions? What if I also told you that this same man is now being told by God to warn everyone that *this day is coming soon?*

The "Day of the Lord" is mentioned many times by Jewish and Christian prophets, yet few understand it. It will be the worst day ever on planet Earth, a day terrifying to those who come to it unprepared. Since *every* prediction in Scripture about events that have already happened has come true just as it was prophesied, it is reasonable to believe this will come true as well. Here are Isaiah's and John's exact words describing this cataclysmic event:

> *Scream in terror, for the day of the Lord has arrived—the time for the Almighty to destroy. Every arm is paralyzed with fear. Every heart melts, and people are terrified. Pangs of anguish grip them, like those of a woman in labor. They look helplessly at one another, their faces aflame with fear* (Isaiah 13:6-8 NLT).

> *Then everyone—the kings of the earth, the rulers, the generals, the wealthy, the powerful, and every slave and free person—all hid themselves in the caves and among the rocks of the mountains. And they cried to the mountains and the rocks, "Fall on us and hide us from the face of the one who sits on the throne and from the wrath of the Lamb. For the great day of their wrath has come, and who is able to survive?"* (Revelation 6:15-17 NLT)

When my friend of many years, David Jones, told me the same vision experienced by Isaiah and John had happened to him, I asked him to describe it. He was there. He saw, felt, and experienced the final day on earth—the Day of the Lord! I want you to know what he experienced and realize what is coming so that you can be prepared!

David is not a psychic and he does not claim special powers, but God has given him accurate visions of things to come. For example, when he was just 13 years of age, he saw his father's death in a motor vehicle accident about a week before it happened. On another occasion he urgently warned a young lady that she must get right with God before it was too late. He later learned that she had died shortly thereafter in an accident. He has since had countless prophetic warnings for others that have proven to be accurate, and now he has a warning for all people.

THE DAY OF THE LORD

David Jones has had two visions that relate to the coming Day of the Lord. The first concerns the event itself, and the second is about when it will happen. David had the first vision before he had even become a believer in the Messiah and before he had ever read the prophecy in Isaiah. Here it is just as he told it to me:[1]

> I was just 17 when I had my first amazing vision of the end times.
>
> I was babysitting my sister's two children one night. It was about eight o'clock by the time I put my niece and nephew to bed. Afterward, I went into the living room, picked up a portable radio, and began to surf the airwaves trying to find something I could enjoy. Not finding anything, I turned the radio off and put it down.
>
> Suddenly, I heard the piercing, high-pitched scream of a woman. Frozen in place and looking all around, I had a hard time figuring out exactly where the sound was coming from. It didn't seem to be coming from any particular side of the house, but rather from the air itself.
>
> As I cautiously moved toward the open window in the living room, I sensed that I was about to see something I didn't want to see. I slowly pulled the

curtain back and peered outside. Was it a woman being assaulted, or even killed, right outside of the house?

But there was no woman in sight. In fact, the street below appeared to be totally empty. It was all rather alarming, and my nerves tingled with the tension of the moment.

I pondered all of this for a moment, then I started to turn away from the window. But something made me turn back, and this time I looked upward toward the heavens. Just when I had begun to feel as if there was really nothing to be alarmed about, a very strange scene began to unfold before me in quick succession. First, a strange-looking moon appeared, and then it actually seemed to drip blood. Then all of the stars began to fall simultaneously from the sky, and the sky began to roll up like a scroll.

After all of this transpired, I saw the woman. She had long, black hair, and she was looking up into the sky, watching everything that was taking place. In horror, she was screaming and digging her nails into her already-bleeding face.

And then I saw the others. At first there were just ten people—men and women—running in fear. Ten became hundreds and then thousands. Everyone was running frantically, hysterically, and falling over each other. As they attempted to get up and keep running, they had a look of utter horror on their faces.

In that moment God allowed me to feel the sheer horror and total helplessness these people were feeling and thinking—that the end of time had come and there was nothing and no one who could stop what God was doing.

Just as suddenly as the vision had appeared, it was gone. I fell to my knees, trembling.

"That had to be my imagination!" I said. "What I just saw could not have really happened." And yet, even as I said it, I somehow knew that what I had just seen and felt was not my imagination. It was all too real.

But what did it all mean? Still shaking, I remembered having seen a Bible in the room. As I moved toward it, fearful that I was about to see more, I begged God, "Please don't let me see anything else!" What I had already seen was more than I could bear. Finding the Bible, I opened it, my gaze fell upon a passage from the book of Revelation, and I began to read:

And I beheld when he had opened the sixth seal, and, lo, there was a great earthquake; and the sun became black...and the moon became as blood; and the stars of heaven fell unto the earth. ...And the heaven departed as a scroll when it is rolled together; and every mountain and island were moved out of their places (Revelation 6:12-14 KJV).

Now I was really scared. I was far from being a believer in God at the time and knew little of the Bible, so I called my Uncle Eddy. He explained to me that strange signs in the heavens would occur just before the judgment of God, the great and terrible Day of the Lord.

The memory of that vision haunted me for years, but it took a near-fatal accident at work to finally wake me up to God and the reality of facing His judgment. When I did finally wake up, I gave my life to Him.

The second vision He gave me of the end times has brought a sharp urgency to my life. In the second vision, He showed me that this great and terrible Day of the Lord is approaching sooner than most expect.

"I Am Coming! Set Your House in Order"

Early one morning in February 2012, while I was still in bed, I felt as if someone had taken my arm and shaken me awake. I was immediately catapulted into an open vision of the future where I was hovering over the earth. At first it was peaceful with beautiful, clear, blue skies. I could see the different ranges of mountains and hills, and all of the people and inhabitants of the earth calmly going about their daily routines.

With no warning at all, the sky turned very dark. Thick gloomy clouds and a deep sense of eeriness quickly overtook everything. With that darkness came a sudden and strange silence. Almost immediately, the silence was broken by a deafeningly loud sound coming from heaven.

It was like seven claps of thunder rolled into one. Never had I heard such a sound in all of my life. It sounded like hundreds or thousands of trumpets, blasting so loudly that it not only pierced the ears of the men and women who heard it, but it resonated in their bones, as well. In response, their bodies shook with the terror that quickly took hold of them.

I knew that this vision was from God; and in the moments that followed, God allowed me to sense and feel what all these people were sensing and feeling. When it happened, they all reacted in much the same way—with a terrible piercing scream. Men and women were filled with sudden terror, shock, fear, and helplessness such as they had never known before. They knew this was the end of time everyone had been talking about.

Next, it was as if someone had taken a razor blade and split the heavens, for here came the Lord Himself with all of His angels, and with Him came the power, glory, and majesty that only God could possess. Oh, such glory—and what beautiful colors! I thought of all of the different shades and palettes of colors I am so accustomed to seeing on the earth— all of the blues, greens, and yellows. But those colors I'd seen with my natural eyes in no way were comparable to the colors that were before me now! These were the supernatural colors of heaven. Such majesty! Such power! Such glory!

As the Lord was breaking through the clouds and coming toward the earth, He was moving so rapidly that people couldn't think. It all happened so fast that I could easily understand why someone who thought it could never happen would be completely taken by surprise. I was seeing it all with my own eyes, and was in a state of disbelief; but it was happening exactly as the Lord said it would.

Many of those who saw the Lord were so frightened they urinated on themselves and shook uncontrollably. There was total chaos and confusion. People were wailing, screaming, and didn't know what to do.

I will never forget when one young man cried out, "No! No! No! No! No! Wait! I thought I had time! I thought I had time! I thought I had time!"

Another cried out, "Oh, no! Wait! This must be a dream! This must be a dream! I will wake up! I will surely wake up!" But he couldn't wake up because he was already awake. It was not a dream—it was the real thing.

All around me people were screaming and running in confusion and terror. Then I heard a voice from heaven saying, "This is the Day of the Lord, for it has come!"

Suddenly time stood still, and everything was about God. No one went to the malls to shop, or to the theaters to see movies. No one was going about their business as usual. Now, for every soul on earth, time stood still, for the hour had come.

This was God's day, it was His hour and somehow everyone knew it. The Messiah had come and

Earth's citizens were totally unprepared for His coming and what it meant for them.

By showing these events to me in advance, the Lord was commissioning me in a very special way to warn all humankind about the coming Day of the Lord. And the warning He showed me was this:

I AM COMING!

I AM COMING!

I AM COMING!

SET YOUR HOUSE IN ORDER!

READY OR NOT...I COME!

When I came out of the vision, I was shaking uncontrollably. I had always considered myself to be such a tough guy, but now I found myself curled up in the fetal position on the floor.

The Lord had catapulted me into the future to show me what is to come for humanity, and I didn't want anything to prevent me from being ready for it.

A CONFIRMING DREAM

This is Sid Roth again. David Jones is not the only one who has received this type of message. All of a sudden, many people from various walks of life are getting the same warnings from God. Even Orthodox rabbis in Israel are saying that they hear the footsteps of the Messiah.

About the same time David had his vision, I had a similar dream. I had not been thinking that the Messiah would come back soon. I knew it was possible, but I thought most likely it would not happen during my lifetime. After all, as I write this I am seventy-three years old. But *all* has changed!

*The Day of the Lord approaches
and we must be ready.*

I recently had a vivid dream in which I was told three times from the Messiah, "I'm coming back soon...I'm coming back soon...I'm coming back soon!"

I awoke with a certainty that the Day of the Lord approaches and we must be ready.

MY FIRST VISITATION FROM GOD

That warning dream was not my first experience with God. I have been a Jewish believer in Messiah Jesus for more than forty years. I became a believer after I had a visitation from God that turned my world upside down. On the worst night of my life I had gone to bed so fearful I didn't want to live. I can't even express how hopeless I felt.

However, when I awoke the next morning, everything was different. My bedroom was flooded with the tangible presence of God. Every cell of my body was invigorated with His life. In this atmosphere of God's love, fear could not coexist. This was life-changing. I instantly knew that Jesus was the Messiah and I wanted to know more of Him.[2]

WHY I CONTINUE TO BELIEVE

People have asked me if I still believe in Jesus as fervently as I did in the beginning. They also wonder if I could have just imagined that first experience of His presence. If that were my only experience, I possibly would have stopped following the Messiah. It is not a very popular thing to do for a Jew, and for a long time it put me at odds with my own family and most of my friends.

However, my faith is stronger now than ever because the Spirit of God literally lives inside me. As I am writing to you now I feel His presence. It's like rivers of living water flowing through my body. It's wonderful, and better than any high someone can have with drugs or alcohol.

I know Jesus as a friend, and in His name I have seen sickness leave people and more miracles than I can count. On my radio and TV shows I have interviewed thousands of people who have had their own miraculous and amazing encounters with Him. I have seen thousands of lives transformed when people come to know Jesus for themselves. My entire Jewish family eventually came to believe in Messiah Jesus.

- He is personal and interested in every aspect of my life.

- He is constantly smiling upon me—24/7.

- He is always happy to see me.

And He is proud of me. Not for what I do but for who I am. I am His son! I walked for thirty years without His favor. And now I am walking *in* His favor. Trust me. His favor is better!

His love is *very* different from human love. He sent His Son to forgive me of my sins *before* I even knew He was real or that I was a sinner. When I had my encounter with Him,

I didn't even know about asking for forgiveness for my sin. I was overwhelmed by His love and He captured my heart. Then I found that the sins I thought were important for my happiness gradually disappeared. Even stubborn addictions could not stay in the presence of His magnificent love.

God has the answer for all your faults and all your fears. Since God is pure love, what He did for me, He passionately desires to do for you!

> *God has the answer for all your*
> *faults and all your fears.*

There is a second powerful reason for my faith, and that is the phenomenal accuracy of the *Word of God* in predicting things that have come to pass. When you open your eyes and heart to the number of Bible prophecies that have been literally fulfilled, you too will feel humbled at the mystery and awesomeness of God.

BIBLE PROPHECIES ABOUT THE JEWISH PEOPLE HAVE COME TO PASS

Although I celebrated my bar mitzvah (when a Jewish boy is recognized as a man), and attended an Orthodox synagogue, I knew very little of the Scriptures. I had spent most of my time in the synagogue reading the prayer book and learning our traditions.

If you asked me if I believed in God, I would have said, "Yes," but I had never really thought about it. God was just not relevant. My life was all about me. I didn't realize all humans are hardwired to know God.

I hadn't studied the universe and comprehended how its complex magnificence proclaimed an intelligent Designer. Did you know that the brain of a honeybee, which is the size of the head of a pin, computes at the rate of *ten trillion* computations per second? How much more intricate is the human brain, let alone the rest of the human body? But all of this proof was lost on me back then.

I hadn't even thought about how many times my life had been preserved in close calls with death or injury. Now that I have thought about all these things, I know they did not come about by chance.

Once I was confronted with the truth, I had to learn more about this God who was pure love.

I devoured the Tenach (Old Testament) and found that it was filled with accurate predictions about the future of the Jewish people, along with hundreds of prophecies about the Messiah that were fulfilled in Jesus.

Since the discovery of the Dead Sea Scrolls in the twentieth century, we have proof that no one has changed any of the ancient Bible prophecies. These predictions written thousands of years ago are so specific and so amazing that it had to be an act of God for them *all* to come true. There are hundreds of specific prophecies that have already come to pass! *And there are hundreds more that will be fulfilled in the near future.*

GOD REQUIRES 100 PERCENT ACCURACY

God tells us how to know if a prediction is from Him. He says that if a prophet makes *one* mistake, the prediction is not from God (see Deuteronomy 18:21-22). After all, there is no such thing as time in eternity. Therefore, God has already seen the event before He dictated it to a prophet who wrote it in the Scriptures. The Bible is made up of thousands of predictions for the future. This is why not one has been wrong!

For example, the Bible says the Jewish people would be the most blessed people on earth and live in the most blessed land on earth, Israel, *if they followed Moses and the Scriptures*. But if not, we would lose our country, many would die, and the rest would be scattered to the four corners of the earth. Whatever country we would go to would eventually turn against us and we would be in fear for our lives (see Deuteronomy 28). *This sad history of the Jewish people has unfolded just as the Bible said.*

But the Bible also says in the last days a nation, Israel, would be born in a single day (see Isaiah 66:8). On May 14, 1948, in one day, Israel was proclaimed a Jewish nation. After thousands of years as a wasteland, Israel became a nation in one day. The Jewish people who were without a country of their own, without a Temple, persecuted and murdered in every country they migrated to, became a nation again! The Jewish prophet Jeremiah said as long as there would be an earth there would be Jewish people (see Jeremiah 31:35-36). Look how easy it would have been for this prediction to be wrong!

The prophets Amos and Isaiah predicted that the Jewish people would return to the land of Israel from the four corners of the earth and that they would rebuild the waste cities (see Amos 9:14 and Isaiah 11:12). Those who returned spoke many different languages and could not communicate with each other. But just as God supernaturally kept the Jewish people as a distinct people group after two thousand years, and formed modern-day Israel in one day, He gave them the pure language of Hebrew as foretold by the prophet Zephaniah (see Zephaniah 3:9). Hebrew is considered a "pure" language because there are no curse words in biblical Hebrew!

These precise predictions and hundreds more came true because God inspired the men who wrote the Bible.

The land of Israel was a barren desert; no one wanted to live there. But the Bible predicted the waste cities would be restored and inhabited. It also predicted the agricultural miracles of modern Israel (see Isaiah 35:1). Centuries before the modern scientific breakthroughs that made it possible, how could Isaiah know that the barren desert would be full of vegetation? The only logical reason these precise predictions and hundreds more could come true is that God inspired the men who wrote the Bible.

PROPHECIES OF THE MESSIAH

And just as God predicted the future of Israel and the Jewish people, He predicted a coming Messiah who would restore humankind's fellowship with God, and told us how we could recognize Him. He said the Messiah would be born in Bethlehem and gave a specific time frame in the book of Daniel (see Daniel 9:25). Did you know that there were several Bethlehems at the time Jesus was born? But the prophet Micah was so precise he said the Messiah would be born in Bethlehem Ephrathah of Judea (see Micah 5:2)!

The Messiah would be despised and rejected by men (see Isaiah 53:3). He would live a sinless life (see Isaiah 53:9). He would be betrayed for thirty pieces of silver (see Zechariah 11:12-13). He would die by crucifixion (see Psalm 22:16). He would have His clothing gambled for at the time of His death (see Psalm 22:18). He would arise from the dead (see Psalm 16:10). And the majority of the Jews would not recognize Him (see Isaiah 53:3), but the Gentiles would follow Him (see Isaiah 11:10). All these things happened.

Moses told us a prophet was coming Who would be like him. He would also come from the Jewish people. That eliminates Buddha and Mohammed. This One would be greater than Moses for two reasons. First, God would put His Words inside of Him. Second, God would require obedience to those Words. Most feel Moses was talking about the Messiah. (See Deuteronomy 18:15-19.)

Actually there are over three hundred specific prophecies about the Messiah that were fulfilled by Jesus! According to the law of compound probabilities, there is only one chance in 33,554,432 that even 25 of these prophecies could be fulfilled by a single person.[3] Jesus fulfilled *27* Messianic prophecies in a single day![4]

My Orthodox Jewish father was taught all his life that Jesus was *not* the Jewish Messiah. However, when he read the following passage from the Jewish Scriptures, written seven centuries before Jesus was born, he was shocked. He knew this passage was talking about Jesus! Before he died, my father received Jesus as his Messiah. Read Isaiah 53 and decide for yourself whether this sounds like a prophecy about Jesus!

> *Who has believed our message? To whom has the Lord revealed his powerful arm? My servant grew up in the Lord's presence like a tender green shoot, like a*

root in dry ground. There was nothing beautiful or majestic about his appearance, nothing to attract us to him. He was despised and rejected—a man of sorrows, acquainted with deepest grief. We turned our backs on him and looked the other way. He was despised, and we did not care.

Yet it was our weaknesses he carried; it was our sorrows that weighed him down. And we thought his troubles were a punishment from God, a punishment for his own sins! But he was pierced for our rebellion, crushed for our sins. He was beaten so we could be whole. He was whipped so we could be healed. All of us, like sheep, have strayed away. We have left God's paths to follow our own. Yet the Lord laid on him the sins of us all.

He was oppressed and treated harshly, yet he never said a word. He was led like a lamb to the slaughter. And as a sheep is silent before the shearers, he did not open his mouth. Unjustly condemned, he was led away. No one cared that he died without descendants, that his life was cut short in midstream. But he was struck down for the rebellion of my people. He had done no wrong and had never deceived anyone. But he was buried like a criminal; he was put in a rich man's grave.

But it was the Lord's good plan to crush him and cause him grief. Yet when his life is made an offering for sin, he will have many descendants. He will enjoy a long life, and the Lord's good plan will prosper in his hands. When he sees all that is accomplished by his

anguish, he will be satisfied. And because of his expe-
rience, my righteous servant will make it possible for
many to be counted righteous, for he will bear all their
sins (Isaiah 53:1-11 NLT).

YOU CAN HAVE INTIMACY WITH GOD!

Just as God told us the history of the Jewish people and how to recognize the Messiah thousands of years in advance, He told us how to experience the presence, love, and friendship of God for ourselves.

God's original intent was to have an intimate relationship with humankind; and in the beginning, Adam and Eve had this kind of relationship with Him. But when they disobeyed God, the beautiful intimacy they had with Him was lost. The subsequent history of humanity has been cursed. When people have not been preoccupied with the pain of hunger, natural disasters, disease, crime, and war, they have searched for comfort through worldly success, money, power, love, drugs, sex, gambling, and a host of other things that always leave people feeling emptier and more lost than before.

There is a God-shaped hole in our hearts that
only God can fill. We are designed to know God.

There is a God-shaped hole in our hearts that only God can fill. We are designed to know God. It is literally in our DNA. There is a way to intimacy with God, and a way to fill that God-shaped hole. God desires that intimacy even more than you do.

The Jewish prophets have told us how to be restored to our rightful relationship with God—we must get free of the sin in our lives. We are told our sins separate us from the holiness of God.

We all sin, but when God forgives us, we are reconciled with Him and we gain the power to be free. Only God can forgive and give us the power to be free. I have met many who have been set free from all kinds of sins, addictions, compulsions, and illnesses through the supernatural power of God.

Now is the time to examine your life and remove any sin that separates you from experiencing the love of God. But you need supernatural help to be set free.

GOD'S REMEDY FOR SIN

Here, in brief, is God's remedy for human sin:

- In the Jewish Scriptures, only the blood of an unblemished lamb sacrificed in the Temple could cover our sins and provide reconciliation with God (see Leviticus 17:11).

- Since the Temple was destroyed in A.D. 70, a New Covenant was needed.

- God predicted this New Covenant by the Jewish prophets (see Jeremiah 31:31-34).

- In the New Covenant, the earlier animal blood sacrifice is shown to be a shadow or foretelling of the blood of Messiah (see Hebrews 10:1-14).

- Jesus is called the Lamb of God, and He is the sinless Passover Lamb that God provided to die in our place and pay the penalty for our sins, which is death.

The New Covenant that was predicted in the Jewish Scriptures would do three things the Old Covenant could not do. This is why it would be called "better" (see Jeremiah 31:31-34):

- First, God said He (His Word) would live inside of us. That's exactly what Moses predicted about the One Who would be greater than him.

- Second, we would personally know Him. The Hebrew word for "know" is the same that is used when the Scripture says that Adam knew Eve and had intimacy with her.

- And third, He would so wipe out our sins that He would remember them no more! This is so much better than only covering our sins as we did in the Temple sacrifices. And because the animal sacrifices that atoned for our sins had to be in the Temple, which is destroyed, the New Covenant is our only hope!

HOW YOU CAN BE RIGHT WITH GOD

The penalty for sin is death, permanent separation from God, and it can *only* be removed by acting in accordance with God's instructions in which an unblemished lamb can die in our place. We must exercise faith in God's provision through the New Covenant. The unblemished Lamb of God who died in *your* place is the Messiah, Jesus.

> *To be forgiven and reconciled with God is to experience His love and peace and friendship.*

To be forgiven and reconciled with God is to experience His love and peace and friendship. This is how to really live for the first time in your life. Are you ready to be forgiven and reconciled to God? Are you ready to have experiential knowledge of God? Are you ready for great intimacy with your heavenly Father?

THE DAY OF THE LORD COMES UNEXPECTEDLY

Remember the people in terror that David Jones saw? They thought they had more time. The Day of the Lord will come unexpectedly and suddenly:

> *But the day of the Lord will come as a thief in the night, in which the heavens will pass away with a great noise, and the elements will melt with fervent heat; both the earth and the works that are in it will be burned up. Therefore, since all these things will be dissolved, what manner of persons ought you to be in holy conduct and godliness, looking for and hastening the coming of the day of God, because of which the heavens will be dissolved, being on fire, and the elements will melt with fervent heat?* (2 Peter 3:10-12)

Note well—that Day will come soon, unexpectedly, suddenly, as a thief in the night. I don't want you to be one of those who cried out, *"I thought I had more time!"* I want you to experience God's love rather than His wrath.

WHAT CAN YOU DO NOW?

I have personally experienced the promise you are about to read from the Bible in my own life. I know this will also be true for you. How do I know this? God loves you as much as He loves me.

The Bible promises that *"If you confess with your mouth the Lord Jesus and believe in your heart that God has raised Him from the dead, you will be saved. 'Whoever calls on the name of the Lord will be saved'"* (Romans 10:9,13).

You would not be reading this book unless God has called you to know Him. God has taken the first step. Now it is your turn. You may or may not feel anything. The feelings and experiences will come as you grow in knowing God by reading the Bible. *Your first step is based on a decision.*

God says,

> *Today I have given you the choice between life and death, between blessings and curses....You can make this choice by loving the Lord your God, obeying Him, and committing yourself firmly to Him. This is the key to your life.* (Deuteronomy 30:19-20 NLT)

Tell God you are sorry for your sins and ask Him to forgive you. He will! The blood of Jesus will wash you clean and God will no longer see your past sin. Now say this prayer *out loud* and enter into the joy of the Lord:

"Gracious God, I am a sinner. Please forgive me for my sins. I believe Jesus died for me and by His blood I am forgiven. You remember my sins no more. I ask You, Jesus, to live inside of me. Take over my life. I make You Lord of my life. Amen."

Welcome into the *mishpochah* (family) of God!

ENDNOTES

1. Excerpt from David Jones, *They Thought They Had More Time: I Saw the Day of the Lord* (Shippensburg, PA: Destiny Image, 2013). Used by permission.

2. To read more about my supernatural encounter with Messiah Jesus and a full presentation of the Scriptures proving the Bible is from God and Jesus is the Messiah, visit: www.TheyThoughtForThemselves.com.

3. See http://www.answers.com/topic/compound-probability.

4. See www.TheyThoughtForThemselves.com/27 for a list of the twenty-seven prophecies that Jesus fulfilled in one day.

About the Authors

Sid Roth is host of "It's Supernatural!" television show and also a prolific writer. Watch archives of Sid's TV show, listen to his weekly radio program, or view his 24/7 *It's Supernatural! Network* at www.SidRoth.org.

Paul McGuire is an internationally recognized Bible prophecy teacher and the author of 23 books such as *The Day the Dollar Died* and *A Prophecy of the Future of America*. Paul is a frequent guest on Fox News, CNN, and the History Channel. H2 Network featured him twice on shows about prophecy. Paul is a professor of Eschatology at Kings College and lives in Los Angeles, California. He is the senior pastor of Paradise Mountain Church International. Contact: www.paulmcguire.us.

Bill Salus is an author, researcher, lecturer, and radio host of the popular "Prophecy Update" radio program heard in Southern California and on his website. Bill is an expert at explaining the prophetic relevance of current Middle East and world events, and his articles have been featured on World Net Daily and elsewhere. Contact: www. prophecydepotministries.net.

L.A. Marzulli is an author, lecturer, researcher, and filmmaker. He lives in the Santa Monica Mountains with his wife of 30 years. Contact: www.lamarzulli.net or www .lamarzulli.wordpress.com.

Perry Stone is founder and president of Voice of Evangelism in Cleveland, Tennessee. He has produced an extensive library of books, CDs, and DVDs, and hosts "Manna-Fest," a national and international weekly television program. Contact: www.perrystone.org.

Mark Biltz, founder of El Shaddai Ministries, is a well-known speaker on the Feasts of the Lord showing how the fall feasts will be fulfilled to the very day as the spring feasts were. He authored the best-selling book *Blood Moons,* that reveals links between eclipses, the biblical feast days, and Israel's history. Contact: www.elshaddaiministries.us.

Dr. Thomas Horn is an internationally recognized lecturer, publisher, and author of more than a dozen best-selling books. He has been interviewed by U.S. congressmen and senators on his findings, as well as featured repeatedly in major news media around the world. Contact: www.RaidersNewsUpdate.com.

Ann Rowan has studied Bible prophecy for almost forty years and has a degree in Theology and Divinity. The impetus for her extensive study was a divine vision she received at age twelve in which she was shown the end of the world. Contact: www.flwi.org.

John Shorey attended Northwest Bible College in Kirkland, Washington. John and his wife, Shawnette, have spent much of their time as children's pastors and as traveling evangelists to children and their families. They currently reside in Arizona. Contact: www.tribulationtruth.com.

Ron Cantor pastors Tiferet Yeshua congregation in Tel Aviv, Israel. He is the author of *Identity Theft* and *Leave Me Alone—I'm Jewish*. Ron has traveled across the globe teaching on the Jewish roots of the New Testament. Several media outlets publish Ron's blog, which can be found at www.RonCantor.com.

David Brennan was born and raised in New Orleans and attended the University of New Orleans, earning a Bachelor's degree in Political Science. He was a Louisiana District manager for the 1984 re-election of Ronald Reagan. Since 1992 he has studied Bible prophecy relating to international issues. He is the author of *The Israel Omen* and other books. Contact: www.IsraelOmen.com.

Pat H. Schatzline is president of Mercy Seat Ministries and author of *Why Is God So Mad at Me?* and *I Am Remnant*. He and his wife, Karen, travel the world as Evangelists speaking about the love, freedom, and power of God. Pat and Karen believe that God is raising up a last-day remnant. Contact: www.mercyseatministries.com.

Dr. Jim Richards is a pioneer in the field of faith-based human development. He believes that people need to be made whole by experiencing God's unconditional love. Jim has been successful as an entrepreneur and has written several books that have sold millions of copies. Contact: www.impactministries.com

Watch Our 24/7 TV Network Wherever You Go!

Download our *It's Supernatural! Network* (ISN) App for iOS and Android devices!

ISN streams over 700 archived episodes of *It's Supernatural!* as well as new original worship and soaking programs, supernatural teaching courses, mentoring sessions and more.

Through the ISN App, you can:
- Stream ISN in HD.
- Watch episodes of *It's Supernatural!* TV on demand.
- Listen to *Messianic Vision* radio broadcasts.
- Stay connected to Sid Roth through social media.

Enjoy a taste of Heaven,
here on earth.

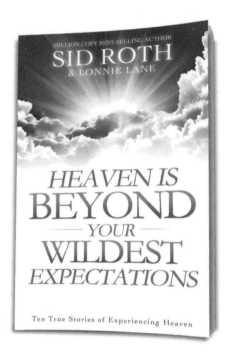

Read the testimonies of ten ordinary people who have been to Heaven and returned, and be reminded that all earthly troubles are momentary afflictions compared to the glory that awaits you in Heaven.

For more information, please visit:
www.SidRoth.org/1512